Fredric Jameson and *The Wolf of Wall Street*

FILM THEORY IN PRACTICE

Fredric Jameson and *The Wolf of Wall Street*

CLINT BURNHAM

Bloomsbury Academic
An imprint of Bloomsbury Publishing Inc

B L O O M S B U R Y
NEW YORK · LONDON · OXFORD · NEW DELHI · SYDNEY

Bloomsbury Academic

An imprint of Bloomsbury Publishing Inc

1385 Broadway	50 Bedford Square
New York	London
NY 10018	WC1B 3DP
USA	UK

www.bloomsbury.com

BLOOMSBURY and the Diana logo are trademarks of Bloomsbury Publishing Plc

First published 2016

Library of Congress Cataloging-in-Publication Data
A catalog record for this book is available from the Library of Congress.

ISBN: HB: 978-1-5013-0833-8
PB: 978-1-5013-0834-5
ePub: 978-1-5013-0835-2
ePDF: 978-1-5013-0836-9

Series: Film Theory in Practice

Cover image: (top image) credit to Peter Rose © APPIAN WAY/ PARAMOUNT / THE KOBAL COLLECTION

Typeset by Integra Software Services Pvt. Ltd.
Printed and bound in the United States of America

This book is for Tim Lee:
"let's go to the movies"

CONTENTS

Introduction

Scorsese/Jameson

Relying on Fredric Jameson's brand of Marxist theory to criticize Martin Scorsese's film about Wall Street would seem to be a gimme: what could be more obviously a capitalist film than one about capitalism? The answer to that question is this book itself, and by way of introducing its argument, I want to first offer a synopsis of the film, then introduce Jameson's system of thought, his ways of reading film and other cultural objects, and finally, drawing on those ideas, situate Scorsese's movie in the context of current films on the economic crisis.

The Wolf of Wall Street begins with a mock commercial for the Stratton Oakmont brokerage that quickly shifts to a dwarf-tossing contest in the firm, followed by a montage of Jordan Belfort's (Leonardo DiCaprio) life: a sports car, model wife, drugs and prostitutes, drunken helicopter rides. Money, Belfort tells us, is his real drug, and we then see the bare bones of his rise to fame, starting with a job where he is taken under the wing of the hedonistic Mark Hanna, who snorts coke at three-martini lunches and suggests masturbation as a counter to the cerebral work of selling stocks. But the crash of October 1989 ends Belfort's first job, and soon he is reduced to working at a penny stock outfit, a "boiler room" operation, out of a Long

Island strip mall. Now his selling genius holds him in good stead for, instead of the 1 percent commission made selling blue-chip stocks, here brokers earn a 50 percent commission. Belfort assembles a team of salesmen from his motley crew of friends: would-be drug dealers and the like, most notably Donnie Azoff. As Belfort's career and corporate success ramps up (even before he sets up his own shop, he is making $70,000 a month), we see him reel in customers over the phone, inspire his sales team with images out of *Moby-Dick*, and, crucially, entertain the workers with weekly scenes of debauchery: half-naked marching bands; alcohol, drugs, and prostitutes; sex in the elevator and exotic pets (boa constrictor, chimpanzee) on the trading floor. Belfort meets Naomi, the "Duchess of Bay Ridge," and they are soon living in a Manhattan apartment complete with a gay butler, then marry in the Bahamas (Belfort gives his wife a yacht called the *Naomi*), and settle into life on Long Island's Gold Coast, Belfort's appetite for drugs and illicit sex not impeded whatsoever.

Attention from outside his circle comes from two directions: first, a profile in *Esquire* magazine gives Belfort the moniker the "Wolf of Wall Street," a name that his friends now call him, but which is also his "safe word" ("Wolfie") in sex games with a dominatrix mistress. But interest in Belfort's unorthodox stock trading is also building with the FBI. This has all taken place in the first hour of the film, its first act, as it were, and the second depicts Belfort's accelerated money-making and money spending, both legal and illegal, simultaneous with increased interest from law enforcement. The center of the film's plot turns out to be an IPO (or Initial Public Offering of stocks) for a shoe company, which, handled by Stratton Oakmont, is also a way for Belfort, via his "rathole" friends who hold stocks illegally, to make 22 million dollars in a few hours. Such profits mean the cash has to be stashed somewhere, and so a scheme is hatched to smuggle it into Switzerland, in luggage or, improbably, wrapped around women's bodies. In the film's final hour/act, things descend in a downward spiral: people are arrested, Belfort and friends endure a horrific storm on their yacht, he is under house arrest, engages in some played-for-laughs domestic violence, and ends up in jail. The film ends with Belfort, as in real life, back on his feet as a motivational speaker.

The film's first message is clear, if ambiguous: being a stock broker is a lot of fun, but are we to disapprove of the lifestyle? This is a common ambiguity to be found in many of Scorsese's films: do we admire Charlie in *Mean Streets* (1973) or Travis Bickle in *Taxi Driver* (1975) or Henry Hill in *Goodfellas* (1990), or do we wag our fingers at their foul mouths, larceny, and violence? Is the libidinal excess of *The Wolf of Wall Street* an indictment of the rich, a post-Occupy Wall Street allegory, a moral critique, or is the film merely a vapid pop culture artifact, complete with the violence, misogyny, and consumerism utterly typical of contemporary American entertainment?

As may be expected, an interpretation of *The Wolf of Wall Street* developing out of Fredric Jameson's film theory will do more than fall into such a dualistic and false debate. Fundamentally, a Jamesonian critique will always be both *immanent* and *symptomatic*. Immanent in the sense coming out of Hegel and the Frankfurt School, which is to seek to interpret a cultural object on its own terms, finding the contradictions inherent in a philosophical or literary project, rather than holding it up to an external standard. Symptomatic in a post-Freudian sense, that reads the film or text for what is repressed or excluded, but not to make a psychoanalytic argument with respect to individual psyches or traumas, and instead with the goal of arriving at a social critique embedded in that film or text. For Jameson, films and other cultural objects always make possible a Utopian critique or account of the historical present. Such an account, Jameson argues, is not so much present in surface readings that are enthralled with what the film wants to tell us as in the film's "political unconscious," in its *non-dit*, its "unsaid," what the film seeks to repress or exclude (or to contain as a form of co-optation).

Thus, Jameson argues that classic 1970s films like *Jaws* (Steven Spielberg, 1975), *The Godfather* (Francis Ford Coppola, 1972), *Dog Day Afternoon* (Sidney Lumet, 1975), and *All the President's Men* (Alan J. Pakula, 1976) are attempts, respectively, to negotiate American postwar history, or to critique capitalism via the mob, or to think about class in our mediatized present, or even to think about global capitalism as a totality via representations of conspiracy. If *The Godfather* was a mob film that was really about corporate capitalism, perhaps *The Wolf of Wall Street* is a Scorsese gangster film in the guise of an indictment of finance capital. And thus Belfort's "crew" of salesmen, many of whom are petty criminals, is not only a kind of heist picture motif, but also an allegory (a privileged technique for Jameson) of the collective, of the possibilities of a class revolt. In addition, Jameson is a key theorist of postmodernism, and so we can see that the film's turn to other media—its incessant use of real and made-up commercials, for instance—is a way of situating the modernist medium of film in a post-cinematic landscape. A media ecology where "immaterial" labor and objects, the existential threat of downloading, and misleading film trailers are the new normal (thus one trailer for the film was scored with Kanye West's song "Black Skinhead," which does not appear in the actual film or on its soundtrack).

A Jamesonian interpretation will find a social meaning in how a film works formally, and this volatilization of the media ecology on the part of *The Wolf of Wall Street* forbids us from falling into what I will call a "laborist-substantialist" critique of finance capital—the argument that whereas factory workers and other blue-collar types actually *make things*, stock brokers merely "push paper" around: it's all "fugazi," or fake. For this last ideology—call it Fordist nostalgia—can evidently be used to disparage many other kinds of labor besides finance capital—from the gendered "pink collar" ghetto of the information and service economies to today's digital, precarious, and affective forms of work. Rather, through its very investment in the "libidinality of the fugazi" (and using investment here in both economic and psychic senses), *The Wolf of Wall Street* helps us to understand better both the crisis and how to organize.

To understand how allegory works in a Jamesonian sense, think of Hitchcock's 1954 film *Rear Window*. Jeff (James Stewart) is a photographer who is laid up in his apartment because he broke his leg taking pictures at an auto race. Everyday he sits at the window of the film's title, watching the bathing beauties and everyday dramas of his neighbors. He starts to think the man across the way (Raymond Burr) has murdered his invalid wife. But no one believes him. Lisa (Grace Kelly), Jeff's on-again, off-again girlfriend, tells him he just offers "wild opinions," his insurance company nurse calls him a Peeping Tom. Lisa asks him, "What are you looking for?" Similarly, his cop friend Tom (Wendell Corey) is unconvinced: "you didn't see a body or a killing," Tom says, "and it is too obvious and stupid to kill your wife in front of all the spectators"; "you saw something," he adds, "for which there is a simple explanation." Eventually, Lisa comes around. "Tell me everything you saw," she says, "and what you think it means."

Now, what the film is evidently doing, and most critics agree with this first premise, is establishing a self-reflexive allegory: Jeff is like a member of the movie audience, and the view out his window is his cinema. We see Jeff looking, then we see what he sees, and then we see his reaction. But if that allegory describes the film's premise as a whole, then this debate between Jeff, Lisa, and Tom can be seen in a more precise way as a struggle for interpretation. The struggle for interpretation, in turn, can be thought of as the primary emphasis of cultural Marxism over the past century: how do we understand cultural objects as a way of better understanding capitalism? It is no accident, for example, that Jeff is not only a photographer, but a photographer who cannot work. That is, his labor is now, for capitalism, useless. And yet he will still use his tools: he often looks at the neighbors through a telephoto lens; he uses his flashbulbs to blind the murderer.

A Jamesonian interpretation of this scene would argue, first, that its formal dimensions—shots out a window in which we identify with Jeff, his increasing interest in the puzzle of the murder—are themselves symptomatic of our alienation from one another, of mid-twentieth-century anomie. And then that turn on the part of cinema to its own allegory would, Jameson argues, tell us something about how we collectively work out, or struggle for, an interpretation. In lieu of a genuine class struggle, mid-century America argues about the movies. We will see how important going to the movies is for Scorsese later in this study.

This argument, this interpretation of *The Wolf of Wall Street*, will be made in finer detail in the book that follows. But it is necessary first to introduce some basic elements in that argument, following the structure of the book series: first, that is, the film theory of Fredric Jameson, and then some opening arguments with respect to Scorsese's film.

Jameson: A brief sketch

Fredric Jameson is an American academic, born in Cleveland in 1934 and educated at Haverford College, where he studied with Wayne Booth, and at Yale, where he worked with Erich Auerbach. Both of these scholars were interested in the forms of narrative: Booth, most famously, in *The Rhetoric of Fiction*, argued that the "unreliable narrator" to be found in the fiction of Henry James meant we should not read the sentences in a novel in a naïve way; Auerbach, in *Mimesis*, tracked the poetics of prose from Tacitus through Boccaccio to Stendahl, always arguing that propensities toward or away from realism were in every way a reflection of the social and political circumstances in which writers worked. This attention to form, born in the indigenous soil of Jameson's education, then was joined to his intellectual interests (themselves prompted, perhaps, by a sojourn in Europe in the 1950s) in the existentialism and structuralism of French philosophy (first Jean-Paul Sartre, then the explosion of such figures as Roland Barthes, Michel Foucault, Jacques Lacan, and Jacques Derrida) and in the cultural Marxism of the Frankfurt School (including its ancestor, Georg Lukács, but especially Theodor Adorno, Walter Benjamin, Ernst Bloch, and Herbert Marcuse).

Jameson's intellectual genealogy can be detected in his first three books, *Sartre: The Origins of A Style* (1961), *Marxism and Form: Twentieth-Century Dialectical Theories of Literature* (1971), and *The Prison-House of Language: A Critical Account of Structuralism and Russian Formalism* (1972). Since the 1970s, Jameson's *oeuvre* has gone in two major directions: thus, he continues to write on and to be a major figure in literary and Marxist debates with books and essays on Wyndham Lewis, Adorno, modernism, Utopian theory, and *The Political Unconscious: Narrative as a Socially Symbolic Act* (1981), this last one of his most influential concepts and, indeed, books. At the same time he has worked in popular culture and postmodernism, writing on Hollywood film (in addition to the directors mentioned, he has also written on Alfred Hitchcock, Robert Altman, Stanley Kubrick, the Wachowskis) but also art films from Asia (Edward Yang and Kidlat Tahimik), Europe (Theo Angelopoulos), and the Soviet Union/Russia (Andrei Tarkovsky, Alexander Sokurov), on the *pulp fiction* genres science fiction and detective novels, and, again with the most influence, in theorizing postmodernism in *Postmodernism, or, the Cultural Logic of Late Capitalism* (1988).

This is a large and sprawling body of work, and the challenge for us here is to determine what strands from it, what of Jameson's arguments, can be most useful in tackling a film like *The Wolf of Wall Street*. In its quickest formulation, we can say that Jameson argues, consistently, that cultural objects offer a Utopian account of the society of their making, a Utopianism that points to a possible future of equality not only by criticizing the inequality of today, but also by detecting, in the very formal mechanisms of those cultural objects, the possibility of a new way of thinking about the world around us. In the "theory" chapter of this book, then, I offer three sets of through-lines for Jameson's criticism. I first look at his writings on film, focusing especially on his writings on popular films such as *Jaws* and *All the President's Men*. I look at two theoretical excursuses of Jameson's, his notions of a "political unconscious" and of postmodernism, then turning to his writings on Utopian theory, closing the chapter with an account of some of the reception of Jameson's theory over the past few decades.

As noted, while Jameson writes on films from different national and regional traditions, I focus here on his essays on popular American film. Scorsese is, as he himself often declares, an American director and therefore a Hollywood director, and it is with respect to the constraints and possibilities of that corporate system, of the films that are produced by that system, that Jameson's theory offers the most profound interpretive argument. Jameson's theory is immanent in the sense that it finds in Hollywood film a dialectic of reification and Utopia. By reification, Jameson means—and he draws on Lukács—how, under capitalism, our relations with each other are replaced by things, by objects, by things that are bought and sold. Hollywood movies are *reified*, are mere commodities, which is an important fact that one should never let go from our sight: they are reified first of all in the sense that they are the result of an enormous amount of collective labor, of material expenditure, of budgets and contracts, and set decoration and phony explosions. That would seem to be self-evident, and yet such material and financial concerns are, it turns out, absent from much film criticism, be it the everyday journalism which focuses on star interviews and weekend box offices, or the loftier heights of academic writing, which, even as it has, in recent years, delved into the "post-theory" realms of national film histories, jettisoned Marxist explanations for the post-political.

A useful reminder of the relevance of financial explanations for filmic product (and one particularly germane to discussing a film about Wall Street) may be the work of Edward Jay Epstein, whose *Hollywood Economist* book depicts in granular detail how Schwarzenegger negotiates contracts, the necessity for film studios to "create" audiences anew for each release, and the effects of a proliferation of distribution forms (thus, for example, the size of the Wal-Mart market means nudity is effectively off-limits for major studio releases).[1] And, again, relevant to our film, Epstein in particular delights in narrating how Hollywood is able to finagle Wall Street hedge funds into what are called "asymmetric deals," whereby "the outside investor gets a smaller share of the total earnings than does the studio on an equal investment," or the story of how a Wall Street consortium lost almost a billion dollars trying to fund a Sony purchase of the MGM studio in 2004 (due largely to changes in DVD sales). As if to confirm Jameson's thesis of a "political unconscious," of the economics of such a repressed in the Hollywood system, Epstein alerts us to the division of budgets into "Above the line" and "Below the line," the former, "ATL," denoting the executive class (producers, directors, "talent" as the actors are known), the latter, "BTL," the labor (makeup and hair, set decoration, creature effects, and the like). Above and below: thus the spatialization of class is allegorized in the very budgeting of (in Epstein's breakdown) an Arnold Schwarzenegger film.

But Jameson's argument with respect to reification is itself dialectical, in that he is making the point that the very *forms* of mass culture—from Hollywood movies to pulp fiction—are themselves a matter of another kind of reification: the repetition of genre. That is, a horror film or a detective novel offers us the security of an expectation, a contractual obligation that the object will not turn into a comedy or a romance. This repetition is a degraded form of the genres of yesterday (the epic, the landscape painting), which existed in a previous historical period, but it is also a dialectical counterpoint to high culture, to the repetition to be found in tedious video art or the insistence-through-repetition of Gertrude Stein.

We must pay attention to the economics of film, as well as to its genres, which have metastasized in the past twenty or thirty years. Horror films, for example, can now be the comedies of the *Scream* franchise (Kevin Williamson and Wes Craven, 1996–2011), the "torture porn" of *Saw* (James Wan, 2004) or *Hostel* (Eli Roth, 2005), or even the self-reflexive horror of *The Cabin in the Woods* (Drew Goddard, 2012). But this attention to the selling of movies should also, for Jameson, be accompanied by an interpretation of the film that seeks out its Utopian message or formal agenda. By this we can understand Jameson to mean two different things: first, a film will engage in a "strategy of containment" whereby it offers, tantalizingly, a Utopian message or possibility thereby to entice the viewer, which will then be of necessity foreclosed or ejected from the film's narrative universe. Then, those very constraints, or hermeneutic difficulties of the film, constitute a signal of the challenges inherent in understanding, and thereby organizing to overthrow, contemporary capitalism.

If Jameson's writings on film offer examples of an immanent critique, his notion of the "political unconscious," developed in the 1981 volume of the same name, is perhaps the most important example of symptomatic interpretation. Thus, it is under the banner of anti-symptomatic critique that Jameson's work has most recently been attacked. As the terms "political unconscious" and "symptomatic" suggest, Jameson here is borrowing heavily from Freudian and psychoanalytic theory. He is arguing that a cultural text will of necessity contain a *non-dit*, an "unsaid," that cannot make its way to the surface.

But where he breaks with the orthodox Freudian tradition (which we can think of in a pop culture way with the classic Woody Allen movies of the 1970s: *Manhattan, Annie Hall*) is his insistence that this repression is political, has to do with social turmoil and trauma, and not merely what happened in an individual's childhood. In this regard, Jameson's theory is closer to that of Jacques Lacan (for whom desire is always the desire of the other, and thus is social; but Lacan, for all his occasional references to Marx, was not a man of the Left), and especially Slavoj Žižek. But this last connection seems to be more one of left collegiality than actual theoretical solidarity: their citations of each other may stand as a screen that obfuscates more profound differences: they are, to use a formulation from Žižek, more of an "empty gesture."

Whatever this Freudian provenance, Jameson's theory of the political unconscious is worked out in a way that draws more generally on structuralist and post-structuralist theory, notably the anthropology of Claude Lévi-Strauss and the literary scholarship of Mikhail Bakhtin. Jameson's theory of the three interpretive levels argues that we never encounter a film or text fresh or on its own: it comes to us "pre-viewed" as they used to say in video stores for used VHS tapes, whether because of its director's or stars' reputations (a Martin Scorsese film, a Leonardo DiCaprio vehicle), its place in a franchise or as an adaptation, and its mediatization (remember Epstein's notion of the "creation of an audience").

If Jameson's political unconscious helps us to drill down in our interpretation of a film, his theory of postmodernism helps us to understand in a broader sociopolitical context the current media ecology in which we watch movies. The essay's nomenclature, "Postmodernism, or, the Cultural Logic of Late Capitalism," contains perhaps the most famous subtitle in academic history. Jameson seeks, that is, to connect the *forms* of postmodernism (self-reflexivity, blurring of high and low, flatness of affect) to contemporary, globalized, information-society capitalism. Neither a vapid celebration of postmodernism nor a Marxist denunciation of the same, Jameson's essay enumerates the features of today's culture (including new forms of spatiality, history, subjectivity) and finds them to be indicative of problems in understanding (and therefore changing) the aforementioned late capitalism. Drawing again on such post-structuralist theorists as Guy Debord and Jean Baudrillard, Jameson argues that our "society of the spectacle" and our politics of the copy or "simulacra" are neither a brave new world of MTV fun (or, we would now say, social media empowerment) nor a superficial distraction from poverty, pollution, and terrorism, but, rather, the very way in which we understand those last social ills.

But this is not to say that for Jameson old-fashioned radical politics are out of the question: hence the importance, throughout his career, of attending to Utopian thought, from early essays on Ernst Bloch in *Marxism and Form* to his use of the concept in his 1970s writings on film, a full-blown book on Utopian theory and science fiction (*Archeologies of the Future*, 2005), and, most recently, a series of talks and forthcoming book on an "American Utopia." Jameson has always distinguished between "secular" and "theological" Utopias, between the Blochian idea that all cultural products contain some secret message about the possibilities of a better way of life or future, and the more programmatic or direct representations of a Utopia that have constituted a literary genre since Thomas More wrote the first Utopia in 1516. But, and not only in *Archeologies*, he inquires into representations of an ideal form of work, into the ways in which Utopias will be spatially constrained in some kind of island or enclave, and at different times will make the rather startling claim that all ideologies are in some way Utopian, whether they seek to argue for a different way of life (and thus are critiques of the present day) or merely depend on a form of hope. That hope may be found, again, in its most unlikely places: and, if more than once, Jameson has argued that the heist picture (or the band of outsiders in the great crime drama *The Wire*) portrays a Utopian collectivity, we should not be too surprised to find a similar crew depicted in *The Wolf of Wall Street*.

When I described this book project to friends and colleagues, a common response was not unlike the opening to this introduction: why would you need Marxist theory to talk about a film about Wall Street? Isn't it obvious? That response is symptomatic, in that we do not care to inquire too closely into what gives us pleasure, or what we take pleasure in denouncing. But the argument that symptomatic readings of the Jamesonian variety are themselves no longer necessary is a larger pattern in recent critiques of his work, which in their most sophisticated forms, claim that the oppression and exclusions of the contemporary, post–Gulf War II culture are too apparent and on the surface to warrant the full arsenal of a complex reading. In such a view, we should take *The Wolf of*

Wall Street at its word (and image), a tale and movie of excess, and we are back at the start, with the Scorsesean ambiguity so much a hallmark of his work.

Crisis? What crisis?

Since the economic crisis of 2008, when subprime borrowing practices, the U.S. housing bubble, and the bundling of those subprime mortgages into an obscure financial instrument called "collateralized debt obligations" combined for a global effect unmatched since the Great Depression in the 1930s, there has been a concomitant explosion of films that seek to illustrate, explore, dramatize, and cinematize on the financial industry and its malfeasance. In their recent book *Cartographies of the Absolute*, Alberto Toscano and Jeff Kinkle survey this "filming of the crisis," remarking on the difficulties of representing, cinematically, the role of finance. It is hard (or maybe just boring with lots of math) to characterize, or emplot, the entity that is "finance capital."

This may be because of the nature of postmodern capitalism, confined as the workplace is to boring desks or cubicles and computers, which Jameson argues are unrepresentable. Toscano and Kinkle range impressively from the 1930s to the present, from Hollywood to art installations, from leftist artworld heroes Alan Sekula and Harun Farocki to the end-credits for *The Other Guys* (Adam McKay, 2010). They often find the crisis, or economic representations, in unlikely places, such as Bush and Obama's televised talking heads that show up in the crime drama *Killing Them Softly* (Andrew Dominik, 2012). Background screens in a film are rather like parenthetical asides in writing; we are not sure if we are to be distracted by them or not. Our authors are particularly trenchant when confronting left fantasies of Fordism, a nostalgia for blue-collar labor of the kind that inflects Michael Moore's work, for instance, but also the theories of radical geographers David Harvey and Neil Smith. In films that take contemporary corporate life as their subject (such as *Up in the Air*, a film about a travelling executive who fires people, which features cameos by workers "downsized" during the 2008 crisis), the refuge of the domestic (family life *qua* fantasy) is often the only alternative to corporate anomie.

The tag team nostalgia of Fordism on the one hand and family on the other conveniently ignores the racial segregation of labor, restricted public life for women, and rigid homophobia that characterizes pre-1960s life in the West, but that nostalgia also in some obscure way connected, first, to representational or epistemological problems of how to know, or to film, the intricacies of the hedge funds, derivatives, and credit swaps that were so much a part of the 2008 crisis and, second, to the question of affect, or the role of emotions, acting or, again, cinematic representation. The credits for *The Other Guys* are a veritable PowerPoint slide show for the crisis, showing particularly well the obscene differences between salaries and other forms of compensation (the ratio of CEO to worker compensation was 19:1 in 1952, 68:1 in 1978, 319:1 in 2010; an NYPD retirement benefit of $48,000 is compared to a CEO benefit of $83 million), but, with the actual scale, sometimes offering nonsensical (or sublime?) comparisons: thus the Troubled Assets Relief Program (T.A.R.P.) bailout authorized by Congress of $700 billion, we are told, breaks down to $2,258 for every person in the United States, or "enough to buy a trip around the world!"

Presumably one cannot represent what one does not understand, and so Michael Moore, in *Capitalism: A Love Story* offers us the spectacle of bankers who cannot explain their own financial instruments (again, there is lots of math); Moore further argues that derivatives and the like are intentionally complex to make them all the more difficult to regulate (a point that Jameson also makes). Toscano and Kinkle are not persuaded: "this unwillingness actually to understand and present derivatives and their role in the crisis, or this feigned ignorance, severely limits one's ability to thoughtfully respond to the crisis both politically and theoretically."[2] But the problem of knowledge here is more systemic: commentators from David McNally to Michael Lewis document again and again how managers would willfully not know what they were selling or buying (how toxic the mortgages were in CDOs, for instance); more widespread on Wall Street was (or is) the susceptibility of research divisions of brokerages to pressure from the trading floor to promote stocks the firm is selling; finally, the rating agencies themselves (Moody's and Standards and Poor) were, metaphorically, bringing a knife to a gun fight: unable to pay their analysts a fraction of what people earn on Wall Street, they could not assess the securities to which they were assigning credit ratings and would not want to, for fear the firms would turn to a competitor.

For Toscano and Kinkle, this unrepresentability of finance is audible in "the wooden asides peppering recent crisis films," which lack the "magnificent psychotic" nature of earlier films like *Network* (Sidney Lumet, 1976). Also a matter of cinematic representation is the issue of affect or what level of manic exuberance (or flat intonation) different films will employ. Whether a matter of nonprofessional actors (as in *The Girlfriend Experience*—Steven Soderbergh, 2009) or, perhaps, actors saying lines they do not understand, this lack of affect is then similar to what they find in an artworld installation, Isaac Julien's *Playtime* (2013).

I agree with Toscano and Kinkle that the difficulties inherent in finance and securities does not mean critics should abdicate their responsibility. And this question of knowability has two further implications: first, that therefore it's all smoke and mirrors, just a con (in the gangsterish language of our film, it's a *fugazi*, a fake); second, that there is an ontological rot at the heart of finance capitalism, a lack not only of morality, but also of reality—which is to say, again, a Fordist misrecognition of the nature of contemporary economic systems. My argument in this book, then, will be that *The Wolf of Wall Street* confronts this misprision, corrects it, and shows us, in an analogous or allegorical way, the very real conditions (if not the cultural logic) of late capitalism.

These themes of representation, affect, and finance, then, which Toscano and Kinkle corral so well in their survey of crisis films (and as part of a larger project that seeks to apply Jameson's ideas of "cognitive mapping" to an understanding of contemporary, globalized, capitalism) can allow me to conclude this introduction with some brief remarks on my interpretation of *The Wolf of Wall Street*. This film is not directly about the 2008 financial crisis, set as it is in the 1990s, and portraying as it does a firm that mostly dealt with penny stocks and used insider trading to illegally profit from overinflated stocks. But the film's indulgence—its characters' indulgence—in the sex, drugs, and other vices of Jordan Belfort and his crew allows it, arguably to make some germane arguments that situate it in that very milieu. In opposition to the flat asides of other films, Toscano and Kinkle mention Belfort's satiric "subversion of the monologue": for whenever Belfort sets out to explain how IPOs work and how he games the system, he will interrupt himself with a "who gives a shit?" knowing wink to the audience. Belfort often addresses his brokers like a coach on game day or a motivational speaker, and so his knowing refusal to explain his system to the audience is telling, to say the least. Early in his career he has explained to him the essential fakery of the trading floor by his mentor Mark Hanna, who says "We don't create shit, we don't build anything," the system is all *fugazi*, "it's fairy dust, it doesn't exist, it's never landed, it's no matter, it's not on the elemental chart, it's not fucking real." But an important plot point in the film overturns this logic: when Belfort and his crew are making millions of dollars illegally, they have to figure out a way to launder the money. Deciding to smuggle it to the proverbial Swiss bank, they try taping it to an associate's girlfriend. Money is a thing, it turns out, after all.

CHAPTER ONE

The Film Theory
of Fredric Jameson

When Fredric Jameson begins *Signatures of the Visible*, his 1990 collection of film criticism, with the astonishing declaration that the "visual is *essentially* pornographic," he might as well be talking about *The Wolf of Wall Street*. Arguing that films "ask us to stare at the world as though it were a naked body," and, further, that "film is an addiction that leave its traces in the body itself," Jameson seems to be offering a program for understanding the hallucinatory sensorama of a typical Scorsese offering. And so the argument of this book in general is that Jameson's theory of film helps us to understand a movie so exuberantly over the top, but which also seems to be a morality tale about that very excess. And yet it is important to keep in mind that Jameson is a political critic, and his argument in the book in which he makes the above claim, *Signatures of the Visible*, is that only by thinking about film in a historical way can we truly understand just how its pornography should interest us.

A political critic, that is, rather than wagging her finger at us and chastising us for our interest in pornography (or Scorsese), instead inquires into the social conditions that make such films possible—and popular—today. What I propose to begin with, then, is to outline how Jameson talks, specifically, about films, and especially (but not always) commercial or Hollywood films: *Jaws*, *The Godfather*, *Dog Day Afternoon*, and a host of other movies from the 1970s and 1980s. These specific ways in which film is historicized (*Dog Day Afternoon* in terms of class conflict in postwar America, or the "retro" film as a form of postmodernism), I then follow with a more theoretical discussion of Jameson's method: how, in *The Political Unconscious* (1981), he developed an influential system for breaking down a cultural object into precisely how its content and form are related to the economic and social conditions of its making (and reception). I then explain what is one of Jameson's great themes, or the argument that any cultural object will, in however unconscious a fashion, convey a Utopian impulse—and that, furthermore, this Utopianism is essential to culture, to why we pay attention to culture, and to why or how culture is never, finally, enough.

First it is necessary to introduce Jameson's work and its place in the contemporary intellectual landscape. Born in Cleveland in 1934, Jameson grew up in southern New Jersey, where the Pine Barrens of the local landscape (made famous recently in an episode of *The Sopranos*) provided a suitable backdrop for reading Faulkner, and the proximity of Atlantic City and Philadelphia made seeing Hitchcock and foreign films a viable entertainment option. He attended Haverford College (where Wayne Booth taught) and Yale (where he studied with Erich Auerbach). He has since the 1980s taught at Duke University in Durham, North Carolina, and before that at Harvard, Yale, and in the History of Consciousness program at the University of California at Santa Cruz.

First known for his introductions to American audiences of the complexities of contemporary continental theory (in *Sartre* [1961], *Marxism and Form* [1971], and *The Prison-House of Language* [1972]), Jameson was a key figure in the growth of literary theory in the Anglo-American academy. His writings combined French structuralism and poststructuralism with a Marxist heritage of critical theory, philosophy, and psychoanalysis.

In *Marxism and Form*, for instance, Jameson surveyed the writings and works of Theodor Adorno, Walter Benjamin, Herbert Marcuse, Ernst Bloch, Georg Lukács, and Sartre (just as he here reprised work on Sartre from his dissertation published a decade earlier, so too would he return to Adorno, in *Late Marxism*, published in 1989). But, as he warned in his introduction to *Late Marxism*, this was not a journalistic survey, with anecdotes or opinions on offer. Rather, it was an inquiry into the relationship between the formal texts of these writers, studying their works as writing, as texts, and not simply containers of ideas. Jameson's interest lay in the political and historical lessons those texts might have for the current situation of 1970s Western capitalism.

This attention to form, and to the politics of form, then characterized the book that, in the 1980s, made Jameson's reputation, his 1981 volume *The Political Unconscious*. This book veritably established the protocols for cultural studies or new historicism in its mapping out of three "hermeneutic levels" (more on which below), or ways of connecting the text to its history, be it at the level of the text, or its relationship to other cultural objects, or as a genre. Moreover, in *The Political Unconscious* Jameson argued that works of culture stage an "imaginary resolution of a real contradiction," a formula we may find useful in considering the financial contradictions of capitalism that *The Wolf of Wall Street* seems to butt its head up against.

The other great text of Jameson's from the 1980s was his essay "Postmodernism, or the Cultural Logic of Late Capitalism," which began as a talk at the Whitney Biennale, appeared in the *New Left Review* in 1984 (I still remember my excitement coming across the essay in my college library's serial reading room, when I was an undergraduate), and was eventually collected into a book of the same name, published in 1991. Even more than *The Political Unconscious*, the postmodernism essay acquired the status of an instant classic. This was for a number of reasons. First, Jameson talked about a wide range of contemporary culture, from Andy Warhol to

Los Angeles architecture, from *Star Wars* to punk rock, from Language poetry to novels about the Vietnam War. This survey thus grounded his speculative arguments: he was not merely talking about a certain novel, or painting, or film. And unlike other critics who discussed postmodernism, Jameson argued that postmodern culture was not merely a *style*, but had to do with the socio-economic conditions of contemporary life: the service economy, the society of the spectacle, finance capitalism. Finally, he broke postmodernism down into such signal features as the erosion of boundaries between high and low culture, the loss of history and turn to pastiche, the rise of theory, and the death of the subject.

While these forays into theory and postmodernism were establishing Jameson's influence, he was also busy writing about films. Even today, in his 80s, he will typically spend a few weeks in Toronto in the fall during that city's film festival, to catch up with the latest in world cinema. These often-occasional essays were collected in *Signatures of the Visible* and *The Geopolitical Aesthetic* (1992), but Jameson's attention to film has continued up until his latest works—in both *Archeologies of the Future* (2005) and especially *Antinomies of Realism* (2014) he will return to science fiction films, or *Inception* (Christopher Nolan, 2010), *Cloud Atlas* (Tom Tykwer, Lana Wachowski, Andy Wachowski, 2012), and the television series *The Wire* (David Simon, 2002–2008). And the same dialectic of theory and pop culture is maintained through the 1990s and 2000s, with books on Adorno, Hegel, and Marx filling out the Jameson canon. But let's turn to his writings on film, first of all, as a way to orient ourselves to what Fredric Jameson can bring to understanding that important art form, beginning with some general propositions about those writings before turning to specific texts.

For some critics, Jameson's turn to history is both too general and too specific at the same time: on the one hand, he offers large-scale propositions about modes of production (feudalism, capitalism, late capitalism) that serve as background to his readings of cultural texts, while, on the other hand, his theory of history is Marxist history (which is to say, dialectical, and so motivated by the insight of *The Communist Manifesto* that all history is the history of class struggle). With respect to film, then, he works in a system of periodization, where capitalism itself falls into three periods of market capitalism (the nineteenth century), monopoly capitalism (the late nineteenth century up until World War II), and late capitalism (post–World War II, until the present day); to these periods correspond (but only in a rough way) the stylistic periods of realism, modernism, and postmodernism.

Most contentious—and useful for our discussion in this book—is the locating of those breaks, especially the break between modernism and postmodernism: was Hitchcock a modernist (as Jameson argues corresponds to the period of the great *auteurs*), or was he a late modernist or even a postmodernist (with, for example, the "screen" that is the "rear window" in the film of the same title providing a frame for the spectator within the film as well as watching it: a feminist case of voyeurism)? This I want to leave as an open question, since I will argue that the same problematic bedevils Scorsese's body of work as well. If this train of thought originates out of Marxism, another key argument of Jameson's with respect to film comes out of poststructuralist theory and feminism: this is the proposition which I cited at the beginning of this chapter, on the essential pornographic nature of cinema. Jameson expands elsewhere, arguing that film entails a "reduction to the body," that thus results not only in pornography but also violence: thus we see not only, throughout cinema, seductions, near-rapes, or extended nudity and sexual intercourse, but also the body beaten, battered, knifed, shot, or torn from limb to limb.

This may well seem like a gross generalization, and yet surely we would not have the film industry occupation of stunt men and women, of stunt doubles, if such a tendency was not so prevalent as to call for its own specialization, training, and career path. (The sexual equivalent to the stunt double might be the prosthetic penis, glimpsed in *Boogie Nights* [Paul Thomas Anderson, 1997].) And so Jameson has recently argued that the action film becomes in some ways just a dull succession of plot points where explosions and threats to the body are a series of intensities, paradoxically contradictory to the temporality of film itself.

To these two themes of periodization and the body we must add or clarify a methodological priority for Jameson; in this book's introduction I mentioned that any theory following his precepts must work both immanently (or following the tendencies and contradictions of a given cultural object) and symptomatically (reading the surface of a text in terms of what is repressed or occluded)—such a program, it should not be forgotten, is always *dialectical* in two important ways: first, it seeks out the contradictions internal to a film and its workings, and, then, in a way that brings us back to the question of periodization, it locates the film or cultural object in a historical context or situation—not the reified textbook history of timelines, great men, or wars and political parties, but rather history as an absent cause, never really present, available only indirectly through what is not possible, what the film cannot think or do or show.

Jameson's film writings

Sharks and the mob

Two essays in the *Signatures of the Visible* are good places to begin our project of understanding Jameson on film: "Reification and Utopia in Mass Culture" (first published in *Social Text* in 1979), and "Class and Allegory in Contemporary Mass Culture: *Dog Day Afternoon* as a Political Film" (which first appeared in *Screen Education* in 1977). Both essays evidently have something to say about mass culture, as well as the specific films under discussion, and Jameson's claims about mass culture are worth examining. In "Reification," he begins with a dialectical argument, contrasting the populists with the elitists. The partisans of popular culture, Jameson argues, believe that we should pay attention to television and films because of their popularity, because going to the movies and watching TV is what the masses do, and so we will understand the popular will. The more elitist theorists argue that only high art is able to transcend the commodification of everyday life, where all cultural objects are produced for a mass audience.

Jameson's strategy is dialectical. He does not simply argue that one position is better than the other, or even that they are opposed. Rather, he points out continuities, family resemblances, and ways in which what we take to be a feature of high culture turns up in low culture, or the other way around. Taking up such topics as commodification, materialization, repetition, and genre, Jameson argues that high art, in its disavowal of cliché or formula, is only reacting to its loss of a popular audience, and so these generic templates then find their home, *for very good reasons*, in the popular. Consider, for instance, genre: why do popular films fall into such predictable categories as horror, thriller, or rom-com? This is because, Jameson asserts, they are the survival of older genres (the epic, the romance). But whereas those older genres were part of a more stable precapitalist world, today's "generic forms and signals of mass culture are very specifically to be understood as the historical reappropriation and displacement of older structures in the service of the qualitatively very different situation of repetition."[1] That is, myths and adventure stories were part of an organic society, one in which chants, songs, and simple tales were a part of everyday life. The life of the commodity and the division of labor are then inextricably linked: just as songs and stories were freely given, so too everyone could and would tell such stories—there was no "profession" of the storyteller, let alone an author or film director.

Jameson argues that if we historicize genre, we see in classical literature and art what was an unspoken agreement, a social contract, between the artist and his or her public, an organic public. That situation has now, with the allure of shiny commodities in the modern (or postmodern) marketplace, become a situation where the segmented markets want something different (your genre, my genre), but also the same thing over and over again (thriller after thriller after thriller). To check the veracity of Jameson's diagnosis, imagine what happens when we think we have gone into a theater for a crime film and we find out it is a rom-com (or the other way around). And if today, four decades after Jameson made these comments, we believe that Amazon's algorithms will protect us from such anxiety, we will have to think about whether *The Wolf of Wall Street* is a tragedy or a comedy.

Jameson then turns to a third possible take on pop culture, but not before making an aside to which it is worth paying our own attention here. He discusses how we listen to pop music, and form attachments to it that may only resurface ten or twenty years later: think of songs from your youth, which, as much as you would like to deny their hold on you, can still trigger a Pavlovian response when you suddenly hear them in a coffee shop. This phenomenon, he argues, means that there is no "original" song or audition of a song, and the same memory complex obtains to film—especially when we think of the various ways in which film is watched today. Not simply the number of screens (and we will talk about *Wolf* in terms of such post-cinema media), but the repetition of viewings that have been possible since VCRs, and then DVD players, came on the scene in the 1980s—as well as the various digital, VOD, and other streaming services. But we have to also recognize how the film is also an adaptation of a memoir—and this "volatilization" of the filmic text Jameson discusses here, as we will later in the present study.

For the reader of this book who comes expecting a Marxist critique of finance capitalism, such arguments may come off as unconvincing. Isn't mass culture simply about manipulation? Surely a film like *The Wolf of Wall Street* wants to distract us from the human cost of finance capitalism by making us envy the heroes, and guffaw at their antics. And this argument appears to be supported by Scorsese's long-time collaborator and editor, Thelma Schoonmaker, who describes the screenings the filmmakers will set up to ensure they have cut a scene to get the right laughs or other reactions.[2] But here, again, Jameson has a dialectical answer, aligning the manipulation theorists (who by definition must deny cultural products—or their audiences!—any agency on their own) to the protectors of culture, the apolitical formalists who merely want to study film as a hermetic discipline.

But the more substantive reply of Jameson with respect to manipulation—a judo-like move that takes a critique and makes it into a victory—is to reach for his Freud, who argues that dreams take our anxieties and make them into palatable narratives the better to let us sleep, and in particular for the psychoanalytic critic Norman Holland's argument that the work of art "manages" our psychic investments. Such psychoanalytic interpretations, bolstered with a Marxist account of how social formations enlist support among their subjects, mean that for Jameson, mass culture is not merely a matter of a distraction from real politics, or a direct form of manipulation, but instead a way in which the social raises the very anxieties it seeks to control, all the better, like an inoculation, to render them impotent. The danger for any ideological project, however, is that the anxieties will resist precisely this kind of co-optation.

How, then, do *Jaws* and *The Godfather* manage our anxieties—or, at least, the anxieties of 1970s filmgoers? In the 1975 movie *Jaws*, three men join forces to stop a shark from terrorizing a Long Island beach: a scientist (Hooper, played by Richard Dreyfuss), a small town cop (Brody, played by Roy Scheider), and a fishing boat captain (Quint, played by Robert Shaw). In Jameson's reading of the film, he does three things. First he deals with how the shark was, in contemporary discussions of the film, seen as embodying all sorts of symbolic meanings, from US imperialism to sexual desire. Jameson's argument is that the very indeterminacy of these meanings, and their attachment to a shark, betrays a conservative viewpoint, whereby that variety of meanings, their polysemousness, is contained by being linked to nature, to a biological entity. Here

Jameson is countering directly not only US Hollywood but also a prevalent theory of 1970s cultural criticism, which held that the more meanings we detect in a work, the more radical it is. Not so, he says: that very "polysemousness," or multiplicity of meanings, ensures that all kinds of interpretations are themselves co-opted by the natural, biological, and apparent inevitability of the shark and the ocean.

Jameson then discusses the main heroes of the film in terms of how they compare to the Peter Benchley novel and their eventual fate. Here he makes two germane points. First, Quint is a modern version of Captain Ahab, from *Moby-Dick* and thus, according to the logic of Melville's novel, must die. But if this is so, why is it that Ishamel, the narrator of *Moby-Dick*, is split into two survivors: Hooper and Brody? Then, he also reads the film's three male figures in terms of class: Hooper is a representative of a decadent European aristocracy (*à la Death in Venice*—although this is more true of the novel than the film); Brody, like all cops, is virtually the only form of American working class masculinity allowed in mass culture; and Quint's New England Yankee stock represents both New Deal *and* Norman Rockwell ideologies.

Finally, the film's shuffling of characters allows us to detect not merely an alliance between law-and-order (Brody as cop) and multinational technocracy (Hooper as apolitical scientist), but one in turn affirmed via triumph over both nature *and* the older America (Quint). *Jaws* thus raises, only to manage, anxieties over a new consumer society, anxieties that are social and historical (and not merely personal or psychological), and thus must be given voice before they are contained. This work of mass culture, Jameson will soon come to call a "strategy of containment," a very powerful theory both of how film works and of how a hermeneutics of film can tell us something about our present situation. But this interpretation of *Jaws* is to read film in terms of its ideological work: Jameson then turns to *The Godfather* to talk about film in a Utopian way. For there is a dialectic at work here: "anxiety and hope are two faces of the same collective consciousness," and so, Jameson writes, mass culture can only serve as capitalism's handmaiden by giving voice to (and then deflecting or distorting), "the deepest and most fundamental hopes and fantasies of the collectivity."

But before that Utopian reading, Jameson offers two prefaces: first in terms of gangster pictures, and then the allegorical reading of the Mafia. The gangster is historicized— from the classic 1930s of James Cagney to the postwar *film noir* loner—to which may be added the tributary stream of pulp fiction, ranging from the Dashiell Hammett and Raymond Chandler heyday to such 1950s imprints as Fawcett books' Gold Medal series. A history which can be supplemented in an intermedial way (the role of *The Sopranos* in bringing these tropes to television), a racialized way (the blaxploitation genre of films in the 1970s: *Shaft* [Gordon Parks, 1971], *Superfly* [Parks, 1972], *Foxy Brown* [Jack Hill, 1974]), and, to combine these, the complicated ways in which 1990s gangsta rap offered a nihilistic turn to hip hop.

But Jameson is more specific, noting that when

> we reflect on an organized conspiracy against the public, one which reaches into every corner of our daily lives and our political structures to exercise a wanton ecocidal and genocidal violence at the behest of distant decision-makers and in the name of an abstract conception of profit— surely it is not about the Mafia, but rather about American business itself that we are thinking, American capitalism in its most systematized and computerized, dehumanized, 'multinational' and corporate form. What kind of crime, said Brecht, is the robbing of a bank, compared to the founding of a bank?[3]

Note the reversal here: all of the psychic investment we make when we watch a gangster film is flipped. We think we are transgressing, walking on the wild side—and it turns out these films have a political subtext. *Even if they are accurate*. This is the important lesson in Jameson's critique: even if every detail of *The Godfather* (and *Goodfellas*, *The Sopranos*, and the rest of the gangster canon) is accurate, the film still serves an ideological purpose: presenting the fantasy that it is ethical malaise, crime and corruption, that bedevils the United States. Again, it is important to note that Jameson's Marxist critique supplants an ethical one, for those kinds of critiques—which argue that *Mafiosi* are evil, that their actions are bad because they are crimes (what is the difference between the Mob's protection and the police force, after all?)—are themselves only a way of ignoring the historical conditions (from mass immigration to urban poverty) that give rise to crime in the first place.

Jameson then unpacks the Utopian message of *The Godfather*—keeping in mind that we are using "message" here in a very different way than Samuel Goldwyn (or the playwright Moss Hart) said, "If you've got a message, call Western Union." That quip warns cultural workers from inserting politics into their art; Jameson's argument would be that politics will be in there no matter what. The Utopian impulse detected in *The Godfather*, then, turns out to have to do with ethnic envy: with the decline of the traditional family in mainstream (which is to say, white) postwar American society. We envy Don Corleone, Marlon Brando's godfather, because of the authoritarian and patriarchal cohesion of his family (remember that in the first scene of the film, the Don hears a father bemoan his daughter's sexual ethics).

I have gone into some depth here in outlining the first of Jameson's critical analysis of popular film in part because his Utopian reading of the relationship between gangsterism and capitalism will be expanded upon in Chapter 2. But Jameson's essay is worth paying attention to for a number of reasons: for the fine-grained way in which Jameson lays out the various theories of mass culture, for the attention he pays to immensely popular films of the day, and for the powerful critiques of contemporary capitalism that he elicits from these documents of the popular.

Pacino on the sidelines

I now turn to another text from *Signatures of the Visible*, an essay that again takes on a 1970s film: "Class and Allegory in Contemporary Mass Culture: *Dog Day Afternoon* as a Political Film." A note on time and history. As I remark above, both of these essays "Reification and Utopia" and "Class and Allegory" originally appeared in academic journals in the 1970s: within a few years of the films that they discussed. If those essays then were collected in book form and published in 1990, and we are now discussing them again in the mid-2010s, then we have a number of different "lags" or time-shifts to account for. But for now I want to emphasize, by perhaps thinking in a dialectical fashion, on the simultaneity of the essays to their "objects" in the first place (which is to say, written in the historical present—thus a footnote to the "Reification" essay dates its writing in 1976—*Jaws* came out in 1975; the two *Godfather* movies in 1972 and 1974); but then the historical perspective that the essays' book publication and present discussion offers—a historical perspective that will turn out to be key to understanding *The Wolf of Wall Street*.

Jameson begins his essay on *Dog Day Afternoon* with two different propositions: the first, the argument that class is no longer a viable way to conceive of social composition in post-war America (whether because of American exceptionalism—the history of the frontier, lack of an organic aristocracy—or the more recent "service economy" and postindustrial consumerism); the second, that the left has abandoned class as a meaningful analytic category in favor of the post-1960s "new social movements" organized around gender or ethnicity. Jameson evidently does not agree with either proposition—he explicitly says that identitarian and generational categories (race, gender, student politics) are, in terms of theory, subordinate to those of social class. This assertion is worth lingering on for a moment. First of all, by *theory*, Jameson means in terms of theorizing social conditions (and not "only in an abstract fashion"); second, his mentioning of the student movement reminds us of how close this essay was written to the 1960s (and even if the post-Occupy critiques of student debt and the tuition bubble are still very recent today, one does not often talk of a student movement); finally, Jameson's closing comments on the practical and political relevance of those social movements attest to the complexity of his position here: a declaration of the *priority* of social class does not *a priori* relegate other struggles to the bottom shelf.

Rather, Jameson is seeking to understand why such struggles should have eclipsed class (and, with the rise of identity politics in the 1990s, arguably continue to do so). That is to say, in many ways, we can see here a "leftist plea for brocialists" in the vernacular sense that that last term is used: a socialism that seems to claim a certain priority for politics based on class to the exclusion of other social intersections, often understood to be one dominated by white, male, Marxists. But, again, this will come to be important in our understanding of *The Wolf of Wall Street*.

As with Jameson's critiques of *Jaw* and *The Godfather*, his account of *Dog Day Afternoon* revolves on a figural understanding of class, for the very good reason that he is interested in the social conditions of class consciousness. If we do not see class anymore—and this is true even more so today, when we think that both a Starbucks barista and a bank manager are "middle class"—then what role can culture play in that possibility for representation? But this figurability means two sets of problems: first, that what the film "seems" to be about, may turn out only to be so much window-dressing; then, the debatable degree to which the class nature of our social reality (or even changes in that nature) will be "detectable" or symptomatic in a Hollywood film.

As an initial foray, what seems to be most promisingly political about the real-life events (Sonny, the bank robber's, popularity with the crowds; his desire to get money to pay for his lover's sex change operation; and the mediatized nature of the robbery *qua* event) turns out to be cancelled out not only by each other but also by the "strategy of containment" by which any marginalized identity or surface politics are co-opted in commercial culture (in a similar move, Jameson will argue that what is good about the film—Al Pacino's Method acting, for instance—is what is bad, while what is bad—or marginal: incidental locations or anonymous actors—is what is more important).

It is important, then, to understand that a Jameson critique will not indulge in the moralistic finger-waving that goes on about "positive images" (of gay or trans characters, for instance) or "narratives of solidarity" that are supposed to uplift the leftist filmgoer and provide a reason to continue to agitate or revolt. Rather, here as elsewhere, Jameson seeks to implacably uncover the possibilities of class in the most unlikely way. For instance, in terms of what Sudeep Dasgupta has called for in terms of "cross-medial" or "trans-medial" studies of television,[4] but also what is now known as "adaptation studies," Jameson considers *Dog Day Afternoon*—again, because of its relation to a "real-life event"—in juxtaposition to film or television genres not indulged: the various documentary and neorealist traditions from Grierson to Vertov, and the (then new) American TV forms of "docudrama," a distant ancestor to what we might now call reality TV.

But it is also a matter of reading the lead character's anguish and pain in terms of a historicization of Method acting as gentrified existentialism (in which case we have a rather banal antihero, caught up in his private lack) and the rather astonishing way in which Sonny connected with the public (both in the film and in "real life"), the film audience, and the feminized work force in the bank. The audience connects because it is living through the inflationary 1970s and the workers because of their proletarianization in the degraded urban outpost of Brooklyn, toiling for a faceless corporation, Chase Manhattan bank.[5]

And yet, still, this is not where Jameson lays his Marxist bet: rather, he says, because of the complex relationship between representation and class consciousness (and especially because class is not a matter of simply different strata in an objective sociology), and because we are dealing with a cultural object, a film, which works with narrative and character and imagery, we need to look at the very margins of that narrative, instead of following who we think is the hero. The film is not one story, and perhaps what happens at the edge of the narrative, in the corners of the picture, is more relevant than the braying scenery-chewing of Al Pacino. Jameson wants to hijack the film, to watch it against the grain.

What he does, then, is to say that *central* to the film is actually the battle for control (for "turf") between the local, NYPD police, and the FBI—a battle signified as much by the opposition between the ethnic, belly-over-the-belt local cops and the cool, sunglass-wearing FBI agents *and by the actors' positions in the Hollywood star system*. We have Pacino as Sonny, Charles Durning as NYPD Lt. Moretti, and James Broderick as the FBI agent. Here, Jameson argues, "one of the most effective things in the film, and the most haunting impression left by *Dog Day Afternoon* in the area of performance, is surely not so much the febrile heroics of Al Pacino as rather their stylistic opposite, the starkly blank and emotionless, expressionless, coolness of the FBI agent himself."[6] Consider this scene between Sonny and Sheldon:

SONNY: You'd like to kill me? Bet you would.
SHELDON: I wouldn't like to kill you. I will if I have to.
SONNY: It's your job, right? The guy who kills me … I
                 hope he does it because he hates my guts, not
                 because it's his job.

This scene is between two actors as well as between a crook and a cop. Jameson's argument, then, is that in watching a film, we are as much watching actorly styles and what *those styles signify*, as we are following a story, rooting for a hero, cursing a villain.

Jameson's argument, then, is that the relation between the actors—Pacino as star, Durning as character actor, and Broderick as TV actor—works as an analogy, mediating between the cinematic representations (FBI/cop/criminal) and a politics of class: a nonantagonistic relation between the multinationals, superseding the national bourgeoisie, all the better to continue to marginalize workers and other social groups. As an example of the cunning reason of history, what is most degraded or superficial about film—the star system, the gossipy world of which actor makes more money or has the biggest trailer on set—turns out to be its way of, in some fitful, and oblique way, conveying a political message.

This is perhaps the point at which to explain a key element of Jameson's method. If, as I have already argued, his readings of film are symptomatic (thus what is in the film stands for something else), and immanent (he takes the film on its own terms), and if his method is in this way dialectical (he brings terms into opposition with each other, situates a film in its historical moment), much of this way of looking at a film is also allegorical. To understand how allegory works in a Jamesonian sense, think back to our discussion of Hitchcock's *Rear Window*. Jeff (James Stewart) is a photographer who is laid up in his apartment: as I argued earlier, his interpretation of the scene in front of his apartment window is an allegory for the cinematic experience. So too, in *Dog Day Afternoon*, we have an allegory at the level of the film's actors and how they stand in for different forces in multinational capitalism, or in *Jaws* and how the characters represent the triumph of technology and corporate scientific knowledge over older American lifeways. But this allegorical reading of film finds perhaps its fullest expressions in how Jameson talks about conspiracy films in his next book.

Before leaving *Signatures*, it is worth looking at how Jameson outlines a history of cinema in terms of the aesthetic categories or eras of realism–modernism–postmodernism, a history of film and the autonomous work of art, in the long essay that closes the volume, "The Existence of Italy" (155–229). Ranging over questions of technology, auteurism, and photography, Jameson maintains at the center of his inquiry the status of realism in film. And all art, but especially film. He provides the first of two semiotic rectangles, explanatory diagrams of the kind to be found throughout the structuralist film critics such as Jameson. Realism must be considered to be a matter of narrative, how a story is told, but also, with film, becomes a matter of genre—the Western versus *film noir*, women's pictures versus the musical, which then must be viewed as a system. The role of technology in film interpretation then comes into a full Hegelian-dialectical reading, where the technology of the wide screen, or film stock, means what we see in a film might have as much to do with those technical constraints/possibilities as some director's great vision.

Referencing Peter Wollen's materialist argument with respect to production—recording/processing/projecting, to which one could add prerecording decisions around set decoration and costuming (note the role of eyeglass design and props in *Tinker Tailor Soldier Spy* [Tomas Alfredson, 2011])—Jameson avers that the process of critics' "materialist mystification" must never be satisfied with the putative materiality of film stock and the like, but must properly turn to praxis, to social institutions.

For Jameson, it is nonetheless important to think about the film director as an *auteur*, the artist in control of his material. Thus, Scorsese, who came of age as the "film school generation" (Lucas, Spielberg, Coppola), was part of the New Hollywood that "rescued" an industry because their ability to connect with young audiences. Jameson wants to provide a historical explanation for this, and so distinguishes the *auteurs* in the 1930s and 1940s (John Ford, Howard Hawks), who through the studio system forged their own style across genres, from their later versions in the 1950s and 1960s (from Hitchcock to Antonioni, but also globally). Then, their young ideologues theorize into being a new auteurism with both the film school generation and their younger "punk" brethren. Or: post-auteur, as witness the "blockbuster, alternative, 3D blockbuster" history of the past thirty years of film. The question of the *auteur* is for Jameson also a question of artistic autonomy, a liberal way of thinking about how film relates to the society of its making. Film also has a capacity, he argues, to capture via its representational structure, Truth, not as a realist aesthetic (or epistemology) but as an Event, the event of the revolution, of history. But still autonomy lingers as a question: for Jameson, the autonomy at the level of a filmic sentence or image, or an episode, within a film, a fragmentation of the film coming from music hall, the melancholy (in *The Wolf of Wall Street*'s case, we will see, paranoia) *flâneur*, and the Hitchcockian thriller-romance (we will think of our film as the hybrid genre the "thriller-bromance").

Cognitive conspiracies

Published in 1992, two years after *Signatures of the Visible*, Jameson's *The Geopolitical Aesthetic* continues his treatment of films of the 1970s—at least in the first part of the latter, on which I will focus here. Specifically, he discusses the treatment of conspiracy in *Three Days of the Condor* (Sidney Pollack, 1975), *Videodrome* (David Cronenberg, 1983), *The Parallax View* (Pakula, 1974), and *All the President's Men*. Jameson's interest continues to be the possibilities of filmic representability—which is to say, how popular entertainment can convey broad historical questions, and especially how to think about vast programs of global domination and control beyond the ken of any individual human. One can imagine how this problem may be useful as a way of coming to terms with the "vast" system that is Wall Street (or capitalism, or the recent developments of finance capitalism): and so it will be pertinent here to dwell on the implications of Jameson's essay.

The first thing to be noted is that what Jameson is not doing here is coming to these films with a predetermined theory as to what they are about; rather, he is trying to suss out what is going on in a small body of work: how space is conveyed, the role of technology, how the individual and the collective are conveyed, the place of allegory and totality. The book's essays were originally delivered as talks at the British Film Institute in May, 1990. The late 1980s and early 1990s were a time of "the end of history," the apparent triumph of liberal capitalism over its social other, communism (in that brief interregnum between the fall of the Berlin Wall in 1989 and the commencement of the first Gulf War and the Balkan struggles). Jameson's thoughts are marked by a historical urgency, and this urgency is no less so for its being worked out in questions of representation: how can, or does, film show us the world?

Thus, he remarks that even our categories for understanding the geopolitical totality (what we now call globalization or even neoliberalism) are suspect. So the technologies of the Cold War (he mentions intercontinental missiles) and the new processes of gentrification cannot simply be conveyed via more accurate maps (a caution worth remembering as we sink into the Google Earth imaginary). But, also, remember Marx's sardonic comment on the French peasantry in *The Eighteenth Brumaire:* "They cannot represent themselves, they must be represented."[7] If there Marx, ever politically incorrect, was pointing out how the rural poor were patronized, here Jameson is trying to understand how the "social raw material" of the lived world (a raw material to which we relate in a psychoanalytic way: it contains our psychic investments but also our Utopian wishes) functions—how we think in a paranoid way about being controlled by the Other, say (the topic of his essays in *The Geopolitical Aesthetic*), or how we think in a libidinal way about money we want to have (the topic of *The Wolf of Wall Street*).

Two further aspects of Jameson's method before looking at the individual films: he is arguing here for a form of *cognitive mapping*, a map that we only consult unconsciously, as if it is forbidden to directly acknowledge the social totality in which we live our daily lives. Jameson's concept of "cognitive mapping" then is a matter of practice, of what we do everyday, but is also in some way unconscious. Just as we may not think about whether we walk to the left or the right when we leave our house to take the bus (we know, without thinking about it, that the bus stop is two blocks north), so we do not think about the world that we live in, even as we navigate it, usually, successfully.

For Jameson, then, we try to understand the world via its objects in front of us—which means that when they appear in a film, they stand in for something else, for that understanding (or that attempt at understanding). And there is always a lag, a "nonsynchronicity," for we are always living in our own childhood, in our memory or history of the past. So, in a film like *Three Days of the Condor* (in which Robert Redford plays Joe Turner, a CIA agent trying to determine the cause behind a massive liquidation of his colleagues), communications technology—from clicking word processors to telephone switching stations—are a cognitive map for our conception of the greater world.

Not because the filmmaker intends that allegory, nor because we consciously understand it to be so. But because this is the world in which we live, where "the scientific machineries of reproduction" *are* our lifeworld. And consider the film's mapping of Turner's adventures as an "informational mechanic," when he learns "the representational confirmation that telephone cables and lines and their interchanges follow us everywhere, doubling the streets and buildings of the visible social world with a secondary secret underground world is a vivid, if paranoid, cognitive map."[8] Jameson's imagery here suggests not only a secret world underlying what is visible on the surface, but a doubling of meaning and cognition that is paranoid but also true.

Now what is interesting here is how Jameson's take on the film then trumps this representation of conspiracy with a more contemporary argument that, by the 1990s, "telephone technology is still marked as relatively old-fashioned or archaic within the new post-industrial landscape," where computers and video screens are "markedly less photogenic." We will come to appreciate, I hope, the key role that telephones play in *The Wolf of Wall Street*, but for now Jameson's point is that this political unrepresentability marks a certain limit to what films can convey, although perhaps we should not rush too quickly into the idea that computer (or digital or internet, to update Jameson again) technology is merely virtual, or, as we say today, in the "cloud." In his recent study *Tubes: A Journey to the Center of the Internet*, architecture writer Andrew Blum takes us precisely into the places where Jameson's (or *Three Days of the Condor*'s) telephone cables are being supplemented with fiber optic cable. He shows us workers on the streets of New York, installing 1,200 feet of that cable, after consulting a map with "thick red lines" showing their location.[9]

But this is not to dispute Jameson's arguments that, first of all, these representations have to do with our cultural and libidinal investments in the objects around us and, further, that the conditions of representability are always historically contingent. For a couple of pages later, Blum describes a meeting he has at the AT&T building at 32 Avenue of the Americas, a building that anchored the first transatlantic telephone cable in 1955. The building continues, as if a ghastly afterimage, to be a communications hub in the internet era, including a television service company, Azurro HD:

> The company's small room was manned around the clock, and when we walked in to say hello, the technician on duty had a movie up on his enormous bank of mission-control-style screens: the 1975 espionage thriller *Three Days of the Condor*. Standing there inside one of the world's great "nexuses of information," we watched for a long moment as the CIA agent played by Robert Redford tiptoed across the plaza of the World Trade Center towers.

Irony is probably an inadequate word for this squaring of the circle of technology and representation: looking for the "real" of the internet and our virtual world, our intrepid reporter stumbles across a high-tech proletarian immersed in a simulacra of an earlier narrative … of a hero looking for the "real" of his virtual world (it is worth remembering that Redford's character began as an analyst, "Condor," reading spy novels to provide ideas for CIA). No, not irony: dialectics.

By "dialectics," I mean the following in Jameson's terms. First of all, that there is a relationship between a film's turn to technology as its content (the narrative of Joe Turner looking through telephone switching stations to follow a phone call) and film itself as a communication medium. The film, that is, is depicting an alternative medium to itself: Jameson will soon argue that any such depiction is itself fraught with antagonism, be it a photograph in a film, or, I extrapolate, film in the "post-cinematic" moment of television commercials that now surround any viewing. Then, as a further illustration of that principle, we have Blum's book *Tubes*, which not only depicts the laying of digital infrastructure that harkens back to Jameson's contention that "telephone cables and lines and their interchanges follow us everywhere," but also shows us the film audience, in this case, a cable network technician, engrossed in watching *Three Days of the Condor*, as if to remember that *frisson* of paranoia.

As Jameson continues to analyze conspiracy films proper, there are three further critical debates worth paying attention to in his discussion of *The Parallax View*: the pathological character, the question of transmediality, and the recent past. In *The Parallax View*, Warren Beatty plays Joe Frady, a reporter out to unmask a corporation that trains political assassins—the Parallax Corporation. For Jameson, a key question is Frady's motivation, which shifts from the "epistemological" (as a reporter, he desires to know) to the "ontological" (he finds out fundamental questions about the nature of the world). This determination on the part of Frady appears at first to be due to his pugnaciousness, his asshole quotient, which is to say, his psychology or pathology. This is Jameson's argument, that the very qualities that enable Frady to pursue the conspiracy (and even to infiltrate the Parallax Corp., to train as an assassin but then to be so framed, in the end), his rebelliousness, also doom him and, in a Kennedy assassination-like finale to the film, allow the authorities to say he acted alone.

But it is Jameson's working out of the historicization of characterological pathology that interests us here, for he refers to the great Marxist critic Georg Lukács on that very problem. Lukács argues that the modern dramatic hero must embody a form of personality not found in everyday life but, furthermore, in that pathological character what seems to be an "excess" is a response, on the part of drama, to the demands of history. Lukács is arguing that modern drama (he originally wrote this in 1909, describing the drama of nineteenth-century Europe as opposed to ancient tragedies) must respond to the contemporary situation (with what he calls "stylization") and yet must be "confirmed"—or *confined*—to the personal, or individual, which is to say the character's psychology. Lukács shifts from *pathos* (rooted in the Greek παθος) to *pathology*: the first is a classical affect or emotion (and rhetorical device), the last is a feature of bourgeois life, of psychoanalysis and private life. For both Lukács and Jameson, what is most historical about the pathological character is how his motivations are made ahistorical, or private. This argument will come to be important for our treatment of Jordan Belfort in *The Wolf of Wall Street:* in what ways do his sexual and other excesses allow us to view him as an aberration, a pathological addict, rather than the logical outcome of late capitalism?

At one point in *The Parallax View*, Joe Frady, having infiltrated the corporation, is given a test or orientation that consists of various film and still images: the reason is to judge his psychological makeup as a potential assassin. Discussing film critics' arguments with respect to the appearance of text, or television, in film proper, Jameson proposes that "whenever other media appear within film, their deeper function is to set off and demonstrate the latter's ontological primacy," or, more strongly, that "film include other media to dramatize its superiority over them."[10] But this assertion—which will come to be an important way of thinking about the transmediality of *The Wolf of Wall Street* (which begins *as a commercial* for the Stratton Oaks brokerage, and uses commercials throughout)— must be tested or disputed. The function of the images in *The Parallax View*, as noted, is, at the level of the film's plot, to ascertain if Frady is suitable assassin material. But at a more critical level of the film—its geopolitical unconscious, if you will—as Jameson remarks, the images assert that American fascism is as native as apple pie. Jameson echoes one of the advertising slogans for the film's posters, which reads "As American as apple pie"—both recall the African-American activist H. Rap Brown's provocative statement, in the 1960s, that "violence is as American as apple pie." So the pack of snapshot images do three things in Jameson's interpretation of *The Parallax View*: they stage an *agon* between still image and film; they mobilize a crude form of psychological testing for the film's plot; and they connote a simplistic political unconscious whereby conspiracies and corporate control (and violence) are truly American.

Jameson returns to this notion of (what I am calling, following Sudeep Dasgupta) trans-medial ontology discussing another Pakula conspiracy film, *All the President's Men*, when he comments on the reporters' tools of their trade, not only their photocopiers and typewriters but especially the detritus: notes written on scraps of paper, bank records, lists and entries, and the like. Again it is the function of these objects that interests me here (and will guide our return to such questions in the second half of this book). For these media objects are now what simultaneously (in the plot) signify the reporters' work, their writing and detection and inquiry, the unraveling of a conspiracy *and* (in the film's 'geopolitical aesthetic') a historicization of that trade, marking a time when journalism was done on paper, when electronic devices, large and small, had not yet invaded the newsroom. Trans-mediality comes to play a similar role in *The Wolf of Wall Street*, combining these two functions from *Parallax View* and *All the President's Men*, so a video of Belfort's wedding (which p.o.v. is part of how we see the wedding celebration) becomes evidence for the FBI agent on Belfort's trail: thus the trans-medial returns from the political unconscious to the plot.

This final entrée into Jameson's analysis of conspiracy film therefore has to do with history, or the recent past. Consider the very material of technology and the newspapermen's trade in *All the President's Men*, where Jameson notes a certain "uneven development" of tech, and so paper slips and credit card receipts share the cinematic space with *The Washington Post*'s modern, open-plan office. In this regard, Jameson refers to the French poet Louis Aragon, remarking that contemporary life is best depicted cinematically with clothing and furnishings that are slightly out of date—since we always live in a world of last year's fashions, a car bought five years ago, an obsolete trinket. For example, when Gordon Gekko (Michael Douglas) is handed an enormous, 1980s-style, mobile telephone upon leaving prison in *Wall Street: Money Never Sleeps* (Oliver Stone, 2010), the laughter that erupts in the movie theater is the laughter of ideology, as we smugly reflect that *now*, in 2010, we have much smaller phones, and aren't we up to date? Who knew, then, that a couple of years later phones would start getting bigger again?

But Jameson's point is an important one, and one with which we can begin to leave his writings specifically on film and turn to the question of method or postmodernism. After wondering if he is being ahistorical in updating Aragon (from the 1920s) or Benjamin (on nineteenth-century Paris) to the 1960s and 1970s, he argues that postmodern film—and the lifeworld it depicts—is concerned with a much more rapid effacement of the past, of the recent past, than previously, with modernism. This speeding up of fashion and obsolescence cycles is not merely a matter of superficiality. For example, a film with a similar sense of the newspaper business's recent past is Tom McCarthy's *Spotlight* (2015), where it is not clear what is the greater tragedy, the Catholic Church's abuse of children or how the internet has destroyed print media. Or think of Ridley Scott's *Prometheus* (2012), which, although a putative "prequel" to his *Alien* (1979), shows crew members with touchscreen devices, obviously more advanced technologically than the DOS computers, with green command lines, in the first film. Jameson draws our attention to such matters of technology and representation, arguably, because such technology is itself an exteriorization of our consciousness, of our understanding of the world. Technology, that is to say, is a materialization of ideology. But the question of how to determine the ideology in a film or other cultural object finds its fullest exploration in the text we will look at next.

The Political Unconscious and method

I began this chapter with a detailed exposition of Jameson's writings on film, looking over his shoulder, as if we were behind him in the movie theater, the better to see in some detail how he makes his arguments about films, representability, and history. Now I would like to step back, and examine in a more extended fashion the assumptions and methodologies that underwrite his work as a whole. In particular, I will break down his arguments on the three levels of hermeneutic interpretation developed in *The Political Unconscious* (1981), and his arguments about postmodernism, first worked out in a talk at the Whitney Museum in 1982, then published in (and rewritten for) various books and journals, under the titles "Postmodernism and Consumer Society" and "Postmodernism, or, the Cultural Logic of Late Capitalism."

Strategies of containment

Much of *The Political Unconscious* deals with literary texts— it is an argument for how to read Balzac, Gissing, and Conrad. Jameson's fundamental thesis (which can without much damage be installed in or transplanted to a text about film) is that narrative (or *Darstellung:* representation) is the fundamental way in which we understand the world. And that narrative, then, can be understood in two different forms of historicizing: "the path of the object and the path of the subject"—which is to say, concentrating on the objective history of social life, factories, towns and cities, or on the subjective history of how we understand or know that history, the concepts and ideas and narratives with which we make sense of that history. This argument of Jameson's is therefore dialectical, for even when it comes to narratives and representations themselves—be they films or books or paintings, in the movie house or the library or the museum—one can discuss the historicity of those cultural objects, of their thingness as manufactured objects and empirically constituted things, or one can discuss how we perceive those objects, the interpretive codes and frameworks we bring to bear, willingly or not.

Thus, he remarks that we never encounter a text fresh, or unread: rather, it is through the sedimentation of previous readings and interpretations (which is what a "classic" is—and so even when we are told, say, that a remounting of a Shakespeare play "brings something new to it," this gesture is only possible because it is already old, calcified, canonized). We know, or usually know, what a Scorsese film is, or why it is important to have seen *Goodfellas* (that tracking shot!), or the famous "you talking to me?" scene in *Taxi Driver*. And, Jameson adds, even if the text (or film) is brand-new, we still carry around with us "sedimented reading habits and categories," an interpretive muscle memory that is both social and individual. Remember our discussion of genre expectations earlier: we watch a film because it is a rom-com, or because we liked the last film the director made. And in addition, we might think of those viewing habits signaled in the movie itself, for filmmakers usually begin as filmgoers. In an interview, Scorsese's editor, Thelma Schoonmaker, notes not only how Scorsese would watch movies over and over again on the local "Million Dollar Movie" night in the 1950s New York of his youth (which showed the same movie twice nightly for a week), but that in the editing suite Scorsese would run Turner Classic movies *as they edited the current film*. But even this anecdote should not make us think that we are engaged in *auteurist* (or even audience-based) criticism here; rather, in the dialectical synthesis of these two essentially private subjects as part of a larger collective project, because for Jameson, the critical act is for the

most part allegorical (remember the *Rear Window* example)—
we always read a book or see a film via an "interpretive master
code"—in this case, that Marxist hermeneutics of Jameson: and
so the book begins with the call to "always historicize!"

This is strong language, no doubt due in part to the same
marginalization of political and class-oriented theory since the
1960s, when new social movements—but what has also become,
in recent decades, identity politics—asserted the priority of
different, non-Marxist approaches. (Later, while defending the
Marxist notion of totalization, he remarks on the importance
of alliance politics in the United States left.) Jameson's
central argument, then, is that a cultural text must always be
understood in its historical context—but the challenge being,
first, to determine the relationship between the work of art and
its historical context and, then, to do so in a way that respects
the "semi-autonomy" of the cultural product. Jameson sets out
to do so in two ways; first, he provides a compelling working
through of rival theories of interpretation—from debates
within structuralism and poststructuralism, to myth-criticism
and psychoanalysis, all the way back to Christian debates
over biblical interpretation. His thesis is that Marxism, as a
method but also as a philosophy of history, must be able to
hold its own with such rivals, and even if some of these debates
must now, over thirty years later, appear to be over, it is worth
lingering on some of the highlights to understand what comes
next: Jameson's own theoretical methodology.

Again, Jameson states his position in no uncertain terms: if
cultural criticism oscillates between formalism (shot analysis or
discussions of lighting) and impressionistic contextualization
(thus "classic" Hollywood understood as an industry), he
argues that only in Marxism do we find a theory or set of
propositions that situates cultural objects in a historical
context without falling into antiquarianism. This last failing—
antiquarianism—in Jameson's terms means a reflexive reference
to current events and the like (thus a film is related to the
Vietnam War or a novel to the financial crisis) that avoids
more difficult questions of *how* those historical events influence

our viewings or interpretations of said works of culture. And Jameson demonstrates this first of all by demolishing the notion that some films are political and some are not, arguing that it is precisely this categorization which works to maintain the illusion that we have a private or personal life, an individual existence, somehow separate from the political maelstrom (which in turn we think of only, perhaps, in terms of electoral politics, or the unnecessary "politicizing" of the everyday when a minority group or social other kicks up a fuss). So Jameson is arguing that interpretive decisions (how should I talk about this film, as the hero's journey or in terms of the lighting?) are related to the social in the very separation of those very critical approaches—a separation that his form of Marxism seeks to resolve. But this is still to have to deal with the relationship between the film and the historical: and here Jameson's method is not simply to argue that a cultural text "reflects" or is "influenced" by its historical context. Rather—and here is where his title concept, "political unconscious," becomes more than a metaphor—he argues that we must understand that a novel or film is not merely caused by or a reflection of its social context. A text works on that context, shapes how we view it, by what it leaves out, or changes, or, indeed, the text produces its context. Occupy Wall Street or the Vietnam War are as much our images of those events—especially, but not only, those of us who did not directly participate in them—as they are the events themselves. The cultural product works with the raw material of its social situation to shape that raw material into a (in our case) narrative, using (but also modifying) the available techniques and forms. This is where Jameson's method will call on formalist criticism, and will be as attentive to style as any enthusiast of *mise en scène*, but with the proviso that there is a to-and-fro between such aesthetics and the historical context, and so, as we will see, the film is seen to be a "socially symbolic act" that does some work of its own on the social.

For instance, a cultural product must be seen as having or carrying an ideological message, ideology understood in the Marxist sense not just as a blatant politics or even false consciousness, but rather a matter of what it cannot say, what it is forbidden to enunciate or show. Ideology is a practice, not just a system of ideas. Ideology is a "strategy of containment." This last phrase or term has already been encountered in Jameson's writings on film and deserves its own full dress rehearsal at this point. The phrase originates in foreign policy debates at the highest level of U.S. hegemony: it was coined by the then-ambassador to the Soviet Union, George Kennan (in a famous 1946 "long telegram," then expanded in an article in *Foreign Affairs* in 1947), who argued that the best way to counter Soviet communism was to stop it from spreading—that is, the "firm and vigilant containment of Russian expansive tendencies."[11] If for US history, then, the term speaks of a certain kind of realist foreign policy, in Jameson's hands "strategy of containment" denotes those forces in a text that indicate a limit, an outside, to the fictional work: the sea in Conrad's novels, the exotic or primitive other.

We will see what strategies of containment are at work in *The Wolf of Wall Street* later in this study, but consider for now what constitutes the "outside" of the film's stock brokerage world—the brief glimpses of the poor (in Jordan Belfort's speeches) or of an uncontrollable nature (as when the yacht hits a storm in the Mediterranean): such outsides suggest a structural limit to the world of coke, hookers, and the hard sell, which the film tries with all its might to avoid. And, it is these very outside moments, the challenges to the ideology of the film, that a Jamesonian critique seeks to unveil, finding them in particular in moments where the work of art breaks down, contradicts itself, stumbles over a character's inconsistency or hastily patches a narrator's voice-over to better hide its own problems of illusion and realism. Such a program appears antiquated in today's "new normal," where such a schizophrenic text (the term Jameson borrows from Gilles Deleuze) could equally apply to the madcap pastiches of Tarantino, the brain-thudding blockbusters of Michael Bay, and, no doubt, the various YouTube and other post-internet forays where individuals post videos of themselves playing games. That is, how does one interpret the ruptures or stumbles of *Jackass* (Jeff Tremaine, 2002), or any other film already premised on a lack of unity or coherence? If *The Wolf of Wall Street*, in all its trans-medial glory, is already an incoherent text, what is the Jamesonian critic's job? This is an important question and will guide our foray into the film in the latter half of this study.

A "political" unconscious, not a Freudian unconscious

But for now it is worthwhile to remain with *The Political Unconscious* for two more arguments: Jameson's historicization of psychoanalysis, and his outline of a three-level hermeneutic. Jameson distinguishes between three different kinds of historical causality: mechanical, expressive, and structural: his point first of all is not to avant-gardely dismiss the first two; he argues that political readings which make topical or allegorical references are not just misreadings, rather, the resistance to those readings is itself political. Jameson's position here works through not only the French Marxist philosopher Louis Althusser, but also Lacan: history is the Real, which is to say not a text, but only available to us as a text. And then within any cultural work there will be a Freudian machinery of condensation and displacement, not merely having to do with the libidinal or sexual but also the political, which must then be mediated, from the social into the cultural. Hence, Jameson's turn to structuralist methodologies (A.J. Greimas, Claude Lévi-Strauss) renders possible interpretations that tilt, like a Richard Serra skateboard park, "into the underside, or *impensé* or *non-dit*, in short, into the very political unconscious, of the text" that self-same structuralism providing a way to find out what a text does not know it is doing, what it tries frantically to hide or deny, what it cannot know, and yet does know, at the same time.[12] So, again, the notion of what the text or film seeks to contain and what it cannot.

Jameson identifies the particular and genuinely new form of Freudian dreamwork as a strategy of containment; therefore, a Marxist criticism methodologically requires a concept of the unconscious, an account of how a text hides or evades its own truths, in order to work out how a text does not simply mean what it says. Here Jameson's turn to the Freudian hermeneutic is important for how he historicizes that method, not only in terms of the Victorian or Viennese particulars of Freud's bourgeois background but, more persuasively, in terms of the reification or commodification of sexuality and desire. So for Jameson, to historicize Freud does not mean offering a potted biography of his education in late nineteenth-century Vienna, his encounter with this remarkable patient or that anti-Semitic obstacle. (In like manner, Chapter 2 will not dwell on Scorsese's upbringing in mid-century New York, or the particulars of his Little Italy *milieu*.) Rather, Jameson teases out the very conditions for the rise of psychoanalysis as a way of understanding human consciousness, a rise itself to be found, like photography and cinema itself, in the ascent of capitalism and industrialism in nineteenth-century Europe. Just as factories replaced workshops and rural peasants were forced to become urban proletariat, so our desires and senses were made into fragmented objects, and our very subjectivity, what it meant to be a person, underwent radical, and irreversible, change. Now, what is most interesting in Jameson's historicization at this point is that he suddenly turns to the notion of the *senses* having a history, demonstrating said theory with a brief excursus into *sight*. No doubt this is because he will turn to such a context later in the book when he deals with Conrad (who famously declared his intent as a novelist was "above all, to make you see"), but what could be a better demonstration of the applicability of this most abstruse theorizing to our object of study, a film? So, to use the sociological theory of Niklas Luhmann, capitalism is characterized by a process of differentiation, or the breaking down of organic activities and ontologies into smaller units (from academic disciplines to film genres, from the fashion industry to foodstuffs): so too our lifeworld, indeed our bodies. Not only do the senses become autonomous actors—for we suddenly see and hear and smell and touch and taste new things, objects, surfaces—but their praxis in turn acquire differentiated processes. This is true for sight, in particular, keeping in mind, again, how cinema and photography are, even as Freud is pioneering psychoanalysis, suddenly magnificent new art forms. Sight is now, Jameson writes, its own autonomous activity, and "it acquires new objects that are themselves the products of a process of abstraction and rationalization which strips the experience of the concrete of such attributes as color, spatial depth, [and] texture."[13] Such differentiations mean that color, shade, tint, brightness, or glare are suddenly freed from their attachment to any object itself, are floating characteristics that, like the buttons on our TV's remote, seem to offer the freedom to reimagine the world around us. *Seem to offer*, because the flickering images of a movie screen or dull clouds of a photograph are at one and the same time part of a new economic order. So Jameson offers a quick summary of the history of painting, but two examples from contemporary visual culture will suffice. Think of the scene at the beginning of *The Wolf of Wall Street*, where Belmont is driving a red sportscar, and says "no my Ferrari was white, like Don Johnson's in *Miami Vice*, not red" and the car in the shot changes from red to white; consider, as well, the videogame techniques of adding "texture" and "skin" to one's character or avatar (as in *Minecraft* or *League of Legends*). In both cases, the acceleration of modernity (or postmodernity, as we will shortly see) entails a further acceleration of the reification of sight and vision.

With Freud, then, Jameson argues that just as sight is now an autonomous human sense, so that members of the bourgeois family, suddenly apart from their *Gemeinschaft*, or organic community, and thrust into the anomie of *Gesellschaft*, impersonal society, sees their desires and sexuality equally isolated, concentrated, and torn out of any wider integration. When sexual desire is so compressed and repressed, it needs must leach into every crevice and crack of social life, Jameson argues, precisely because it has been excluded. Of course, we are now far from the repressive Victorian scene in which Freud worked and thought, and so we have to reboot Jameson's theory for our post-twentieth-century filmic text. What is so scandalous about *The Wolf of Wall Street* is how it reveals that for these lubricious stock brokers, these bro's, sexuality has little or no exclusion from the social field. Drugs and sex are as much a part of office life as phone calls and sales talks—or so it might appear. For some of the tension or pseudo tension in the film comes from conflict over precisely this issue.

In any event, Jameson does not make the mistake, common to many defenders and critics of Freud, of supposing that it is *sex* that lies at the core of psychoanalysis: rather, it is desire, or wish fulfillment (which is also key to Jameson's argument with respect to the Utopian impulse, as I argue below). Again, Jameson denotes a historical marker for this sudden importance discovered in, as he puts it, the "metaphysics of desire," connecting it first of all to the contemporaneous nineteenth-century critiques of value to be found in Nietzsche and Weber, and to the ongoing abstraction of means and ends, self and environment, and to which we might add, in the case of Marx, use value and exchange value. The problem that desire poses at this stage for Marxism, however, is that it remains petrified, in the category of the individual, a bedrock of liberal or bourgeois ideology that he seeks to transcend with his theory of the collective. But while Jameson does make some nods in the direction of Lacan here, there are ways in which to conceive of the role of desire in a more social, or collective way, that perhaps only became available to cultural studies once Slavoj Žižek began his important synthesis of Lacan, Marx, and Hegel in the late 1980s. For Lacan, desire is always the desire of the other—whether conceived as the "little o" other of one's neighbor or comrade, or the "big Other" of authority figures, the state, the boss, or the father. We have a complicated relationship to our desire, and to the objects of our desire, Lacan argues, precisely because it is tied up in these intersubjective relations—we want to be desired by the other, to desire the other, to have the same desire as the other. And this social notion of desire is what is mobilized or demonstrated in

The Wolf of Wall Street with the sales pitches and speeches that pepper the film like so many irruptions of desire.

Interpretive horizons

Jameson's major achievement in *The Political Unconscious* is still to come: now he will make a detailed argument for a method with which to provide "the ultimate *semantic* precondition for the intelligibility of literary and cultural texts"—that is, he will provide a framework by which one can make sense of a cultural object through its enrichment of a series of interpretive horizon. The first horizon—or "concentric framework," as Jameson calls them—refers to the political and current events that mark the appearance of the cultural text: strikes, revolutions, wars, but also the social history of the family, ethnic struggles, or protest movements. Then, in a longer *durée* or span of time, society conceived of in a properly Marxist fashion as a class struggle (so more absolutely antagonistic and dialectical than the mélange of events and newspaper stories of the first framework). The final horizon is total history, from the earliest, primitive, or prehistoric times of communal living and the slaveholding ancients, through such modes of production as feudalism and capitalism, on to some future, still unimaginable, of socialist or communist equality.

In a sense, what we have here is a zooming out, from a tight close-up (with the film considered as part of its everyday life and politics), to a medium shot (where the film is considered as its own activity, as a statement in the political struggles of the era), and finally to a long or establishing shot (where now we have the greatest "scope" for thinking of what role films, in their genres and forms, play in human history). For Jameson, at each level we have a different kind of "text" or cultural object to consider. At the first level, it is the text itself as work of art, but here thought of not simply as a cultural object to be analyzed for its meaning, and instead conceived of in terms of what it does, as a symbolic act. This idea of the *work* of the text

Jameson develops by reference to the anthropologist Claude Lévi-Strauss. In a famous essay on the Caduveo aboriginal peoples of Paraguay and Brazil, Lévi-Strauss noted that their facepaintings—beautiful, delicate traceries on children and adults alike (the Caduveo were actually adverse to childbirth, practicing abortion and infanticide to such a degree that they could only "reproduce" by abducting children from neighboring tribes)—were a way of working out social inequities—in Lévi-Strauss' famous phrase, they were the "imaginary resolutions of a real contradiction." This notion of culture (and, especially important for our purposes, visual culture) Jameson then takes as a working principle for how, still at this first level of cultural interpretation, the text (or film) works with the raw material of its social context.

Two related caveats are prompts that come to mind here: the postcolonial notion that, surely, Lévi-Strauss (and then Jameson) is displaying all the arrogance of the triumphalist Westerner who, coming across a charming tribe of savages, "deciphers" their backward practices in ways not available to the primitives. And, then, that this practice is only symptomatic of the problem of the "political unconscious" at large, which as an interpretation again suggests that there is more going on in a text or film than its creator knew or intended.

In terms of the first objection, one can point to the long and respected career and work of Lévi-Strauss, who always displayed the highest level of respect for the aboriginal peoples with whom he worked and learned; thus his notion of the "savage mind," while using a term that has fallen out of favor (the book opens with the phrase drawn from Balzac), was precisely to argue that primitive peoples' epistemologies and philosophies were in every way as complex, and perhaps more complex, than the moribund and enervated theories of the West.

As to the second criticism, in the case of film in particular, an art form dependent on so much collective effort, from the labor of production to the processes of test screenings and (often unwelcome) contributions of funders and producers, it is at least conceivable that what ends up on the screen is hardly under the control or intentionality of one director or *auteur*. As well, in a more philosophical or hermeneutic vein, as Jameson argues in response to his own question, the very abundance of signs, meanings, interpretations, and messages that permeates our media-saturated society means that any given text is liable to any number of critical viewings hardly under one individual's control. And this is also Jameson's argument with respect to representability: *because* our "society of the spectacle" is so inundated with images both positive and negative, low-res and HD and 3-D, that very saturation makes any individual image or image-narrative (which is to say, film), only interpretable in the widening of semantic horizons posited in *The Political Unconscious*.

Jameson then turns to a second level of the text, and its work, where the cultural object is thought of in terms of a class struggle at the level of language (or, let us say here, images). Class here is understood not simply as a matter of status or levels—but in an antagonistic fashion—and the cultural object is thought of in a dialogic way, one that both incorporates other cultural objects and texts into itself and also functions as what he calls an "ideologeme," or a basic unit of ideological discourse. So, to take these units of analysis one by one, first of all the class struggle—a key marker of Marxist critique!—that the film partakes in has both to do with its representations of class (always problematic because of the image saturation noted above, in our explication of Jameson's essay on *Dog Day Afternoon*), and with how the film functions in terms of class notions of culture. Then, to think of the history of film in terms of a dialogic struggle is not only to remember the constitutive tension in film studies itself between film as a popular art form and its ossification into canons and art cinema, but also, then, to think of how Scorsese's films fall into (but also trouble) such genres as the gangster film. It is possible to argue for the existence of a certain "ideologeme" of "gangsterism"—a Robin Hood complex for twentieth-century America. Here, Balzac's famous quote that behind every fortune is a crime (cited, incidentally, by Mario Puzo at the beginning of his novel

The Godfather), is turned around. In *The Wolf of Wall Street*, behind the crime (money laundering) is a fortune. And for Jameson, an ideologeme is either a "pseudoidea" (gangsterism as a way of abjectly excusing violence) or a "protonarrative, a kind of ultimate class fantasy about the 'collective characters' which are the classes in opposition."[14] Like genres themselves, which survive from their precapitalist form in the categories of film today, ideologemes offer the viewer a degraded picture, a crude narrative that is all the more satisfying in its simplicity.

More on the ideologeme of gangsterism later, but we still must outline Jameson's third level of analysis, which takes the cultural object to the horizon of human history at its greatest level, the history of modes of production, or the succession of social organization from the most prehistoric (and perhaps communal) hunting and gathering to ancient civilization (which culminated in the slaveholding form), and then from the feudal arrays of Europe to the development of early capitalism and the absolutist state (and the large-scale assault of exploration and colonialism), through to the industrial revolution and its present day "late capitalist" or neoliberal formations. When relating a cultural object to such a large-scale narrative, it is important first of all to distinguish between the modes, means, and relations of production: the first relating to the distribution of economic or surplus value (slavery, feudalism, capitalism), the second to the power structures by which such distribution takes place (the matter of who owns what: classes), and the third to the actual machinery, farms, computers, and other material that are harnessed for that production. And then, as we have already seen with Jameson's keen eye for technology and the differences between, say, telephones and computers for a filmic representability, we can fine-tune this history of modes of production by considering the cultural object at this third level, which Jameson argues should be seen in terms of its "ideology of form," whereby the cultural object is a barometer, that registers several levels of signifying systems.

The third and final level of interpretation (or "semantic enrichment") means two things at once, then: the cultural object, its form, is itself thought of in terms of conflictual registering and haphazard—not to say random—processes. Form is never a sleek, self-confident presentation, even though it may present itself as such. This very conflict is then deciphered as telling us something very important about the historical situation—again, conceived at the highest level, of modes of production. This last situation has something to do with finance capital, that special case of late capitalism or neoliberalism. The historical period that *The Wolf of Wall Street* treats may be an interregnum, lying between the "origin" of neoliberalism (in the rule of Reaganomics and Thatcherism) and its more recent dissolution into the high frequency trading (HFT) and algorithmic brokerages of the new millennium. But, again, such a reading is only possible by paying attention to the *form* of the film, to, I will argue especially, its reliance on the trans-medial as a "shock doctrine" of post-cinema. These last concepts, the trans-medial and post-cinema, which will be developed more thoroughly in Chapter 2, owe their provenance to Jameson's attention to technology, to the antagonisms between a photograph and a film (as in his discussion of *The Parallax View*). They denote the way in which films increasingly are surrounded by and incorporate other rival, media, from CGI to social media—think of Ariel Schulman and Henry Joost's *Catfish* (2010). But, too, films and filmgoing are under existential threat from streaming services and the ubiquity of screens, due both to online piracy and the various sizes of pictures a director must now anticipate.

Postmodernism

In the past few pages I have had to awkwardly move between "text" and "film" as I adapt Jameson's theory of the political unconscious to prepare for its present use. No such transcoding will be necessary in looking at the next text of Jameson's, for his writings on postmodernism have of necessity themselves sprawled over any number of cultural forms and media, from film and literature to architecture, art, and music. As we will see, it is precisely such a heterogenous body of material that Jameson argues characterizes the postmodern epoch. Now, as is appropriate for a text that has, since the 1980s, taken on a canonical status in cultural studies, Jameson's writings have approached the same volatilization that he diagnosed with respect to mass culture. To speak of the Jamesonian archive, then, is to note that Jameson's writings on postmodernism were first occasioned as a talk ("Postmodernism and Consumer Society") at the Whitney Museum in the fall of 1982, and published in the Hal Foster-edited *The Anti-Aesthetic* in 1983; a more extended version, "Postmodernism, or, the Cultural Logic of Late Capitalism," was published in the *New Left Review* in 1984; a text combining these two essays, but with the former title, then appeared in the collection *Postmodernism and Its Discontents: Theories, Practices* in 1988 (and was in turn reprinted in *The Cultural Turn: Selected Writings on the Postmodern, 1983–1998*), while the *New Left Review* essay appeared as the opening chapter to the book *Postmodernism, or, the Cultural Logic of Late Capitalism*, in 1991. This is simply to note first, the variable ways in which Jameson made his arguments with respect to postmodernism, and, then, how that argument has in turn been disseminated.

Postmodernism and cultural studies

Jameson's essay does a number of different things. First of all, it situates postmodern culture in relation to the economic, to what he variously calls consumer society, or post-industrial society, or late capitalism, or globalization, or neoliberalism. As we have already seen, this is a key theoretical or methodological move intrinsic to Marxist theory, which argues that there is a relationship between the economic base of a society and its cultural superstructure. But just as important to Jameson's work as his connection of postmodernism to late capitalism

is his delineation of the features of postmodernism itself—
every step of the way, he not only demarcates what constitutes
postmodernism, but also argues for how that is a sign of
consumer society, the society of spectacle.

Nonetheless, the argument can be broken down into four
very clear sub-arguments or logics: first, that postmodernism is
a break with modernism; second, that it necessitates an erosion
of the boundaries between high and low culture; third, that it
is characterized by the death of the subject and other notions
of affect or personality (including the triumph of pastiche over
parody); finally, that postmodernism can be thought of as the
attempt to think historically when that conceptual skill is no
longer available to us—trapped as we are in a society saturated
with images, all we have is a "nostalgia for the present."

The argument that postmodernism is a reaction to modernism
seems fairly commonsensical, and Jameson was not the first
to make such a connection (the *Anti-Aesthetic* collection, for
example, contains essays that work out that relation fairly
specifically in terms of sculpture and photography). But it also
reflects a historical or social ageing of modernism itself: what
once was terrifying in Picasso or Joyce had, by the 1970s or
1980s, been gentrified and domesticated, canonized in the
museums and in the academy (but also the marketplace, so
Mondrian images were on shampoo bottles, T.S. Eliot was
available in paperback, and Van Gogh's paintings were fetching
in the millions). Finally, as noted above, it is important to keep
in mind the range of cultural objects that Jameson treats here,
how he moves from poetry to painting to film to architecture.
In this regard, the essay is a key document in the discipline of
cultural studies, which seeks both to examine different cultural
works, and to do so in a politicized context that breaks down
distinctions between high and low culture.

Here two further arguments should be worked out, one to
be found in Jameson, and one perhaps not. In an extended
comparison of Van Gogh's painting "A Pair of Shoes" (1886)
to Andy Warhol's "Diamond Dust Shoes" (1980), Jameson
finds a sea change in both technique (from painting to the

various screen-printed images) and message (Van Gogh's melancholic identification with the peasantry—but also the countryside—versus Warhol's cool, x-ray vision of death and consumerism). Emotions now no longer have any depth, are more like a kind of intensity (a word important to Lyotard, but also Deleuze). Jameson also comments that there are as many postmodernisms as there are modernisms, and it is worth remembering that modernism did not just signify the canonical—the Joyce, Picasso, or Stravinsky—but also included many dissident strains, including the urban/noir/pulp varieties (Raymond Chandler, Döblin, Brecht, the entire *film noir* tradition), the Harlem Renaissance and any number of regional or transnational variants, and more avant-garde formations such as to be found in the poetry of Gertrude Stein and Louis Zukofsky.

The collapse of high and low culture would seem to be such a given in the twenty-first century that it is worth looking back at a moment when it seemed to be new or in itself shocking. That erosion of barriers is part of Jameson's own methodology or rhetoric in the various instances of this essay, which all begin with a barrage of names, styles, and objects, from Warhol and L=A=N=G=U=A=G=E poetry to punk rock and the architecture promulgated in *Learning from Las Vegas*. But of particular importance to Jameson is the discovery—which we have already seen him discuss with respect to the volatilization of the object—that academic skills must also keep up with this change: those acquired (say) in close reading poetry or deciphering an Orson Welles film will not necessarily help you with music videos or graffiti. In particular because those skills were often designed to maintain a barrier between high and low.

Jameson also notes that at that particular juncture in the 1980s we had seen the rise of cultural theory (in which I have already argued he was a key player), replacing not just philosophy, but also the disciplinary distinctions between philosophy, political science, history, and literary criticism. But it may be more accurate to say that this was a dialectical process, of simultaneous differentiation and *de*-differentiation: at the same time that disciplines were and are collapsing into one set of theoretical precepts (so one may read Jameson or Badiou or Butler in a film class, art school, or political science seminar), the disciplines themselves have opened up to any number of sub-programs and approaches, from the various ethnic and queer studies programs that gained traction in the 1980s and 1990s to more recent forms of digital humanities and cognitive approaches.

At the start of an essay on Hitchcock in *Signatures of the Visible*, Jameson talks about reading a work of film criticism (by William Rothman) and being aware of the different view of film that he will necessarily have as he peers over from his disciplinary location as a literary scholar. This certainly sums up the postmodern condition of the intellectual, who always must "catch up" to the debate in a neighboring discipline, asking the political scientist or film scholar down the hall for a recent article (or link), the better to escape the closed hell of one's own "field of study."

One of the most *bravura* passages of Jameson's postmodernism essay lies in its analysis of architecture, of the Westin Bonaventure hotel in Los Angeles. At first glance, taking a luxury hotel as an object for cultural critique would seem counterintuitive for a Marxist theoretician: such spaces are merely sites for wasteful conspicuous consumption. Jameson argues, however, that in both its exterior cladding (a mirror skin that reflects downtown L.A.) and interior design (a lobby with vertiginous escalators and elevators), the Bonaventure proposes a new kind of spatial experience. In this "hyperspace," movement itself is a self-reflexive gesture, as walking is replaced by what the architect (Michael Portman) calls "people movers," the elevators and escalators that propel us into a future we can hardly understand, a future that is as spatial as it is temporal. Jameson's argument, then, is that postmodern space overwhelms us cognitively and therefore politically. The elevators and hotel offer no ready connection between our bodies and the built environment: that disjunction is then sign of our concomitant *political* incapacity "to map the great global multinational and decentered communicational network"—which is to say, global capitalism today.[15]

It is here that Jameson first develops a concept we have already encountered in his writings on film, "cognitive mapping," borrowed from the urban geographer Kevin Lynch. But he also turns, for another example of this immersion in postmodern or hyperspace, to Michael Herr's account (in *Dispatches*) of riding in helicopters during the Vietnam War, "we could have choppers like taxis," Herr writes, and "the hundreds of helicopters I'd flown in began to draw together until they'd formed a collective meta-chopper, and in my mind it was the sexiest thing going."[16] Riding in a copter like a taxi, riding in a transparent elevator that shoots you above the city, these paradigmatic postmodern experiences of space demand a new cognitive map, a new knowledge of the world.

Postmodernism has also seen a different kind of subject to go along with the dissolution of academic and artistic disciplines and the constructions of new kinds of space: the decentered subject, the death of the subject, the postmodern or multicultural subject, a subject less given to parody than to pastiche (along with its techniques of appropriation, cut and paste, or quotation—or sampling). This last string of affects and devices is one of the most apparent cultural features of the past thirty years: from architectural quotation to hip-hop, from digital mash-ups to Tarantino, from the Baudrillardean simulacra to the "cloud," we seem to be in a virtual environment of copying, anoriginality, and endless variations on the same.

But Jameson locates the origins of this, again, in modernism, where a high value is placed on authenticity and distinctive styles, from Faulkner's or Woolf's sentences to Orson Welle's cacophony of sound and shots.

Such a notion of artistic style in terms of authentic and private languages was tied, Jameson reminds us, to a notion of the individual self, but also to a sense of a standard of language from which such styles deviated. Hence, the modernists Faulkner or Picasso were easy objects of parody.

However, in the contemporary period, there is such a plethora of subdialects and slangs, of jargons and specialized languages in different vocations, communities, and subcultures, that there no longer exists a standard against which to judge deviation. Pastiche, then, is a form of copying but without a satiric impulse, and can range in social and cultural forms from Judith Butler's notion of gender as pastiche to the Baudrillardean simulacra, the digital copy with no original, the internet as a vast copying machine. If this tendency is then accelerated by the technologies that have emerged since Jameson's essays in the 1980s—the great explosion of the internet and the digital—one must also acknowledge that the desire was already there, in the analog 1980s and 1990s, when Public Enemy or Wu Tang Clan were copying or sampling 1970s soul and funk (or directly from kung fu videotapes), or in Tarantino's riffing off of French versions of American *film noir*, in drag queens appropriating pop simulacra of women's fashion and celebrities or in photographers staging versions of film stills (Cindy Sherman), the racialized archive (Carrie Mae Weems), advertising (Richard Prince), art history (Jeff Wall), or photography itself (Sherrie Levine).

So, this desire for pastiche Jameson connects to the newer forms of subjectivity brought about by or characteristic of postmodernism: with the dialectical twist to inquire as to whether the "death of the subject" announced by poststructuralism (Michel Foucault's "death of man," or Roland Barthes' "The Death of the Author") is the postmortem on what was merely contingent to a certain period of capitalism—since the nineteenth century say—and now that kind of bourgeois subject is extinct, like dinosaurs or the dodo. Or, perhaps there never has been such a subject, it has always been an ideological mystification, a fantasy. But whichever model one holds to be true, this is also related to our lack of a historical sensibility: if there is no more inventing new styles (postmodernism is not only about the modernist break with the past, the rupture, but also the failure of the new), then in some ways we are doomed to keep recycling the past, and so cultural products, like other commodities, endlessly repeat their own successes (and failures), and this "imprisonment in the past," as Jameson puts it, is not the genuine sense of history, rather, it is history as a compendium of styles that can in turn be quoted at will.

Postmodern film: Recycled remakes

Such a notion of an ahistorical historicism, if you will—an era which sees more and more historical novels or historical films as if trying, in vain, to grasp the past but without the cognitive tools to do so (because our media and our lifeworlds keep us always in the consuming present, supplemented by a fetish for the past in all its artisanal fakery) means that we can close this consideration of Jameson and postmodernism with his comments on a certain style of film: the nostalgia film, or what in France was called *la mode rétro*. The style is to be found in both Hollywood and art cinema, in *American Graffiti* (George Lucas, 1973) as well as *The Conformist* (Bernardo Bertolucci, 1970) and perhaps reached its fullest flowering in the 1980s and 1990s Hollywood, with not only *Body Heat* (Lawrence Kasdan, 1981), which Jameson discusses, but also (to list just a few) *Raiders of the Lost Ark* (Steven Spielberg, 1981), *Romancing the Stone* (Robert Zemeckis, 1984), *Back to the Future* (Zemeckis, 1985), and *The Grifters* (Stephen Frears, 1990).

While Jameson conducts bravura analysis of individual films (*Body Heat*, and later in the *Postmodernism* book, *Something Wild* [Jonathan Demme, 1986] is coupled with *Blue Velvet* [David Lynch, 1986]), I want to finish this section with his comments on, of all the unlikely nostalgia films, *Star Wars* (George Lucas, 1977). Of course, the film (and by this both Jameson and I mean "the original," but we will come back to this question) was not about our own past—although it does begin "a long time ago".... Rather, Jameson says, it evokes the serial movies of the 1930s: those featuring Buck Rogers and Flash Gordon, or leering villains and damsels in distress, locomotives rushing down on women tied to train tracks and cowboys to the rescue (and it is worth noting that these films of the 1930s and 1940s were as far back, for audiences in the 1970s when *Star Wars* opened, as that decade is from our present). *Star Wars*, Jameson asserts, "satisfies a deep (might I even say repressed?) longing to experience them again:…the adult public is able to gratify a deeper and more properly nostalgic desire to return to that older period and to live its strange old aesthetic artefacts through once again."[17]

That is to say, for Jameson what was remarkable about *Star Wars* was how it played to two audiences simultaneously. The young could take the film straight, as an adventure story, a space opera. Older viewers, however, could also view it as a nostalgic return to their own childhood, not only in terms of the episodic structure of the film, but also for how it returned them to a structure of feeling for what it meant to watch movies in the 1930s and 1940s.

Jameson's historical question of how films satisfy our needs to relive the past is worth returning to if we think about how films themselves become objects of nostalgia, how they repeat themselves, or are repeated. We can distinguish the most conventional of repetitions, the sequel or the remake, from the purest kind of repetition, the re-release, and a late-comer to the question of repetition, the reboot. The remake has been around since the beginning, or almost the beginning, of film: consider that John Huston's *The Maltese Falcon* (1941) was the *third* adaptation of Dashiell Hammett's novel, or that Billy Wilder's *Some Like It Hot* (1959) was not only a remake of Kurt Hoffmann's *Fanfaren der Liebe* (1951), but also that Hoffmann's film in turn was a remake of Richard Pottier's *Fanfare d'Amour* (1935). And then within this species of repetition, we also have to distinguish between the film that remakes another film (as in *Some Like It Hot*), and the film that takes on the same original, or source, material (*The Maltese Falcon*), and, on a more technical level, the remakes that aim at a pure, or shot-by-shot remake, as in Gus van Sant's remake of Hitchcock's *Psycho* (1960, 1998) or Michael Haneke's of his own *Funny Games* (1997, 2007). From these remakes we can then move on to the sequel and the prequel, or films that then become a series (also known, in current Hollywood industry jargon, as franchises). Here, even the actor playing the hero does not have to be the same (most famously, the half dozen or so James Bonds), and so the character, like the story, survives only as a ghostly image, a degraded copy of a Platonic ideal.

But if the remake and the sequel are well-established Hollywood practices, we also should consider the re-release and the reboot. A more rare occurrence, the re-release will see a film play again in movie theaters, sometimes tied to a DVD release (as with *The Godfather* and *Star Wars*, both of which played in theaters in the 1990s). Here the film itself is an object of nostalgia: "See it again the way it was meant to be seen" was an advertising slogan for the *Star Wars* re-release. And, this nostalgia is itself secondhand: the audience is as much made up of those who never saw the film the first time around (were too young) as those revisiting their memories. Such large-scale events (or attempts on the part of the Hollywood media machine to make a re-release into an event) are also part of the ecology of rep house and second-run screenings that continue with such latter day cult films like *The Room* (Tommy Wiseau, 2003). (The original rep house or cult house film was, according to Umberto Eco, *Casablanca* [Michael Curtiz, 1942].[18]) Although rep and cult screenings in the 1960s and 1970s were in reaction to television, here you could see a film on a large screen and find cinema (be it arthouse, foreign, or experimental) otherwise impossible to view, with rep and cult screenings today, while the screen size and communal atmosphere stay the same, there is hardly ever a question of obscurity: most films, it seems, are available online.

In the same contemporary media ecology we find the reboot, or the tendency, mostly to be found in the superhero and comic book genres, to go back to a hero's "origin" (Spiderman bit by a radioactive spider, Batman witnessing his parents murdered). This is usually in the guise of a new director/star/atmosphere, most notably, *The Dark Knight* reboot of Batman, which drew on the artwork and plots of the Frank Miller graphic novel.

But in all of these cases, we can argue, following Jameson's own comments on *Body Heat*, that "the word *remake* is, however, anachronistic to the degree to which our awareness of the preexistence of other versions…is now a constitutive and essential part of the film's structure."[19] This is another example of what Jameson calls pastiche: films not only refer to other films, but also carry our awareness of their earlier iterations (if only by *The Dark Knight* not being anything like Michael Keaton's Batman, or Heath Ledger's makeup as the Joker so much more crazed than Jack Nicholson's, for example). And if a re-release allows us to see on the big screen what previously we had only watched at home or on our laptop, all cinema in the theater now carry the memory of the home movie experience: who sitting in a cinema has not had that twitch, as we try to pause the movie so we can take a bathroom break? That last form of muscle memory means we have to add a third, and final, supplement to Jameson's theory of nostalgia. For Jameson, nostalgia films return us to the "feeling" of a certain decade or time in the past via the surface of costume and set, but also of the viewing experience itself (audiences watching *Star Wars* in the 1970s were regressing to their childhoods, in effect): and this is a poor substitute for genuine historical memory. Then, I argue, the films themselves have become their own objects of nostalgia, accomplished via re-releases, sequels, reboots, and remakes. Finally, the technological situation of post-cinema, where we are as likely to watch a film on our computer or tablet as in a theater, means that when we do visit a cinema, we are now, via our own body's memories, nostalgic for our own advanced technology. Following this logic, then, the advertisements in the cinema asking us to turn off our cellphones are a feint on the part of the post-cinema present: act as if you do not own that device. Pretend it is the past, before the internet, before you could download films at will.

Postmodernism: Coda

In 2013 Jameson returned to the theme of postmodernism with an essay in the *New Left Review* called "The Aesthetics of Singularity." Now, he declared, historical time (which he had thirty-five years earlier debunked as unrepresentable in postmodernism) was little more than a matter of "singularities of the present," for not only was the past not thinkable, nor, any more, was the future. Rather, we are presented with a series of events, which he connects not to Alain Badiou's influential theory of the Event, but, conveniently for our purposes here, to that unusual financial instrument called the "derivative."

In some ways unknowable (this epistemological problem will turn out to be important in *The Wolf of Wall Street* as well), derivatives are singular, Jameson argues, because each instrument is set up in a unique way. This means that such instruments are resistant to regulation, but also that "the postmodern text—to us a more neutral term than work—or the postmodern artistic singularity-effect, if you prefer, is of the same unique type as that unique one-time financial instrument called the derivative."[20] And there are two lessons to be drawn from Jameson's analysis here: first, that we must be able to connect cultural objects—texts—films—to the contemporary structures of finance capital; second, this becomes even more complicated when, as in this book, we are looking at a film which itself depicts those very workings of finance.

Utopia

In the introductory remarks to his 2006 book *Archaeologies of the Future*, Jameson entertains the possibility that we are trapped not only in our historical present, but also in the remains or traces of the past that linger. This will remind us immediately of his conviction, expressed in *The Political Unconscious*, that a work of art is, at its ultimate level, related to the historical via modes of production and that, further, this has to do with ideologies of form, with the aesthetic conditions of the cultural object. Now we have to consider whether those relationships (of art to history) are a constraint in some way, and, further, to wonder if the contemporary historical moment—say, neoliberalism, and more specifically, finance capitalism—puts a limit onto what a given film can express or do. Jameson's theory of Utopia is first of all a hermeneutic: this is primary both in the sense that such an argument is evident in his earliest discussion of Utopianism—with respect to the philosophy of Ernst Bloch, in *Marxism and Form*, and in the sense that any interpretive act, any attempt to understand a cultural (or political) object is at the same time Utopian. Here, after a brief return to *The Political Unconscious*, I want to concentrate for the most part on how Jameson treats Utopia in his 2005 book *Archaeologies of the Future* (with occasional reference to *Marxism and Form*).

Bloch, Utopia, and ideology

When Jameson treats the theme of Utopia in *The Political Unconscious*, the infiltration of Freudian theory into his Marxism means that the dialectics of Utopia and ideology are thoroughly intertwined. Thus, first of all, each and every cultural object must contain some Utopian impulse—affirming Bloch's theory that even advertising and other detritus of mass culture somehow must make their appeal to us. That Utopian kernel is the lure or the bribe that convinces us to read this novel, watch that movie, or buy such and such a soft drink. That insight is probably inoffensive to most of us, and a wide swathe of cultural studies over the past thirty years has found all kinds of positive politics in music videos, action films, soap operas, and graphic novels. However, it is not just culture which is Utopian, since for Jameson, even the "effectively ideological" proposition is also at one and the same time "necessarily Utopian." These fragments demand a careful parsing, especially of the modifiers ("effectively" and "necessarily"), as well as a careful understanding of the "ideological." The "effectively ideological" is, again, not just your everyday leftist bogeyman. Ideology, as Terry Eagleton has forcefully argued in his book of that title, is all too often just a code word for what we do not agree with, a politics or other system of obvious partisanship (as when, in electoral politics, Donald Trump or Barack Obama are denounced as "ideological"). But when Jameson calls ideology "effective," he is acknowledging that the ideological is successful; for instance, following Bloch, Jameson will detect Utopia in Nazism (but also in bathroom plumbing). One of the most powerful iterations of this decoding of a Utopian impulse comes when, in the *Principle of Hope*, Bloch discusses the Ku Klux Klan, arguing that they are a sort of reactionary distortion of the brigand and other tales of outlaws (Bloch refers to the *colportage* or the cheap chapbooks which feature such tales). Such outlaws and petty criminals are of necessity Utopian, for "[e]very adventure story breaks the moral commandment 'Pray and work'; instead of the first cursing prevails, instead of the second the pirateship appears."[21] If Bloch's analysis convinces, then the KKK and other fascists are that ideological cheap copy, a diversion of the spirit of hope into spiritless dress-up, complete with hoods, as mocked in *Blazing Saddles* (Mel Brooks, 1974), *Django Unchained* (Quentin Tarantino, 2012), and, in a different register, Andre Serrano's 1990 series of *Klan* portraits.

To return to film, then, *Star Wars* is able to capture our imagination with its mash-up of Roman imperial history and Buck Rogers-style space opera; and, further, this success of the ideological is also (and because?) it is *necessarily* Utopian. *Star Wars* is able to do so because it contains or performs a Utopian truth, a Utopian kernel of a resistance to Empire. (This last Empire now denoting what, following Michael Hardt and Antonio Negri, we recognize as the latest version of a postmodern, globalized, neoliberalism.) So, we have a strong form of dialectics at work in Jameson's formulation here: culture is effectively ideological, in that it contains a form of mystification as to how power operates; but it is also, for all of that, of necessity Utopian.

This intertwining of Utopia and ideology also has lessons for us as cultural critics: Marxism must never, Jameson continues, be satisfied with debunking, with a negative critique, with simply an ideological analysis. A negative hermeneutic, he tells us, must be accompanied by a positive hermeneutic, and therefore we must be able to detect Utopian impulses in the most degraded of ideological works of art. This is evidently the method or theory behind Jameson's essay on *Jaws* and *The Godfather*. And yet, Jameson is also severe enough a critic that he will turn this dialectic around, as if the barrel of the gun now faces his own method, arguing soon enough not only for the ideological nature of all culture, but also that, *contra* the "political unconscious," ideological distortion remains even in the Utopian interpretation of a novel or film and, finally, that domination is present in any aesthetic object we encounter.

That rejoinder to our earlier discussion of *The Political Unconscious* is not, however, the end of what Jameson has to say about Utopian inquiry, and in *Archaeologies of the Future* he outlines in the most thorough fashion his ideas of a Utopian hermeneutic. Here Jameson discusses the varieties of Utopianism, especially the programs (whether in Utopian literature or politics) as well as impulses in the Blochian sense. He also touches, throughout the book, on Utopian ideas of what work is—what our investment is in our labor, and whether we enjoy it. This is how we think of everyday life, but also the notion of hope—can we enjoy without hope? Can we hope without enjoyment? What is the role of envy in all of this? And if the tradition of Utopias, since Thomas More, has had to do with space, with what Jameson identifies not only as the island but also the enclave, it also has not a little to do with time, with our ideas of history and also of the future. Under the iron umbrella of Utopia, Jameson also treats issues that are closer to our own film's themes, including the Utopianism of hucksterism, of money (or the wish for its disappearance) and of crime. Throughout all of this, he is still dealing with the Utopia of hermeneutics, of possibility, of the possibility of, perhaps, a film that stages its own contradictions, its own paradoxes, its own, dare we say, dialectics.

The obvious Utopia

Jameson begins *Archeologies of the Future* with the strong argument that to think in a Utopian fashion today is to offer an alternative to the unrelenting drum roll of neoliberal capitalism. Timely and untimely at the same time, it reaches back (the epigraph is a quote from Ezra Pound's 1948 poem *The Pisan Cantos*) while also, in the reading I bring to the text, looking forward to the economic crisis of 2007–2008, via *The Wolf of Wall Street* (but also Thomas Piketty). And so Utopia is immediately a problem, a problem of interpretation, which is not to say the difficulty in detecting the (Blochian) impulse, but the difficulty when there is no difficulty, when the text seems self-evidently Utopian. Noting that Bloch's hermeneutic entails finding Utopian impulses in the most unlikely places (the KKK, for instance), where it is unknown even to its participants, Jameson wonders if texts or events that are on the surface Utopian must then mean there is "something even deeper and more primordial?"

Turning back to psychoanalysis, Jameson refers to "the same hermeneutic paradox Freud [was] confronted with when … he finally identified one obscure aboriginal tribe for whom all dreams had sexual meanings—except for overtly sexual dreams as such, which meant something else."[22] This then is another dialectic, and perhaps it is a development of the relation between Utopia and ideology, as argued in *The Political Unconscious*. So, the Utopian hermeneutic is devoted to finding Utopianism where it is least suspected, in ideology, in the most odious expressions of political hatred, or in films about Wall Street. And while its instruments are precisely those developed by Jameson in *The Political Unconscious*, those devoted to symptomatic readings, what tools can be used when a Utopian meaning is on the surface?

Jameson offers a solution to this problem in marking a distinction between Utopian programs (plans, usually political, for a new society) and Utopian impulses (more subterranean, as we will argue exist in *The Wolf of Wall Street*). Jameson develops this distinction in *Archaeologies of the Future*, enumerating the features of Utopian programs, including the abolition of money, the liberation of women, and the resolution of the contradiction between work and leisure. But now the problem is that such features of the Utopia themselves are only negations of the here-and-now. We live in a cash-nexus society, women are viewed in objectifying and economically restricted ways, we have to give up our free time to work for an income: those features of today, then, seem to determine what is possible even in their mirror image, in their reverse form as a Utopia. It is as if, Jameson remarks, the aspects of Utopia are simply a reversal or negation of the world we already live in, and so they could as easily fit into a political pamphlet. So, these programs are not the core of the Utopia—rather he says, we must turn to the idea of wish fulfillment.

Jameson argues—and he does this specifically with reference to a film, to Jean Renoir's *La Règle du jeu* (1939)—that the work of art "remains a wish fulfillment" which, if it is to be successful *qua* art, must not be a narcissistic fantasy, but must rather (or also) be relevant to the other (which is to say to the audience). And Jameson aligns the very aesthetic quality of the film with its ability to elicit our pleasure, drawing on Freud's comment that, in contrast to daydreams, the recital of which is always boring, the artist "bribes us by the purely formal—that is, aesthetic— yield of pleasure which he offers us in the presentation of his phantasies. We give the name of an *incentive bonus*, or a *fore-pleasure*, to a yield of pleasure such as this."[23] Note that the economic language used by Freud here—bribes and *incentive bonus* indeed! Freud—or Jameson—is almost insulting, comparing the aesthetic pleasures, the Utopian pleasures, of a work of art to the time-and-a-half you get for staying at work after your shift has ended, for working on a holiday or over Christmas.

A little later in *Archaeologies of the Future*, Jameson seems to be declaring the opposite, arguing that seeing Utopian theories as only negative or critical ignores debates within the tradition over the relative value of happiness and freedom. This notion of a more positive function of Utopia deserves exploration, not only to debunk the myth of leftist miserablism, but also to come to understand what is so joyful—or at least fun—to watch in *The Wolf of Wall Street*. You do not have to want to do Quaaludes to enjoy seeing Belfort and Azoff get up to their hijinks (as a matter of fact, you probably won't want to …). But to miss what is essential in a film like this is to miss, perhaps, also to see what is politically progressive about it.

For Bloch and Jameson, the Utopian impulse is above all a matter of hope. And yet, finance capital is never far from their minds—Bloch, for instance, argues that it is only the likelihood of a "Black Friday," a stock market-like crash in fortunes, that deters the ordinary from turning criminal.[24] Thus, science fiction models of communication, Jameson remarks, seem like nothing else than the rhetoric of capitalist exchange, while recent Utopias are delirious in their hyping of profit, for, he admits, hope is the emotional base of the crudest cons and "hucksterism," and it behooves Marxism to confront the likelihood that we all possess a deep affinity for the possibility of a quick buck, or at least we envy those who can do so.

Hope and envy, these conjoined twins, underwrite two of the more startling declarations or findings in Jameson's text: first, the various Utopian projects over the years which declare the need for the disappearance of money (and it is curious that he does not mention Ezra Pound's fondness for Major Douglas' "social credit" scheme), and, then, what also seems to be a natural result of money, the pursuit of crime. The desire to do away with money, and the criminality that chases that same money, we will return to when we discuss the film more thoroughly, but Jameson does provide us with the insight that money itself is already disappearing of its own accord in finance capital, along with, interestingly enough, ideology itself. Here Jameson stays with the hermeneutic problem of how to symptomatically read what is already on the surface (Utopia as a program rather than an impulse)—remarking that ideology has been replaced by "cynical reason," or the surface claim that, after all, one is only after the money, and so needs no deeper justification. This "immanent activity" of moneymaking needs neither the future nor an ideology of the future, and yet will still have one. Thus, envy returns in the form of crime, and the future, but as a disruptive futurity.

I should add here, as a side note that follows up on this question of crime, a commentary on Jameson's essay "Realism and Utopia in *The Wire*"—because one of the first arguments he makes in that essay is that both "sides" of the criminal–police divide in the series are engaged in Utopian enterprises. Thus, on the side of the police, the gathering together of misfits and mutts (alcoholics, dead beats, nepotistic appointees, a political time server) as a way of actually pursuing crime displays what is "a virtual Utopianism, a Utopian impulse, even though that somewhat different thing, the Utopian project or program, has yet to declare itself."[25] Then, the criminals, led by Stringer Bell, will start to reorganize their "business" more profitably (and we are already deep into that interpenetration of business and criminality, thanks not only to *The Wolf of Wall Street* but also to Jameson's reading *The Godfather*). But there is a larger Utopian program at work in the series as well, or rather a series of such programs, from Frank Sobotka's plan to resurrect the waterfront (but via smuggling pay-offs) in season two to the "Amsterdam" drug zone in season three, the cop-turned-teacher (Pryzbylewski)'s interventions into "teaching for the test" in season four, and McNulty's serial killer simulation in season five. In all of these cases, the subterranean Utopian impulse of the wiretapping unit's organization and the criminal gang's profit-seeking—which is, so to speak, the fundamental Utopianism of the television series (along with its formal premise of precisely this mirroring of cops and robbers, a new development in the American *policier*)—then rises to the surface, with such explicit plans and projects.

This "breaking through" of Utopia will, Jameson argues (to return to *Archaeologies*), be a disruption, "the name for a new discursive strategy," which is to think of there being an alternative, rather than the planning out of same. Disruptive futurity is thus both Utopian impulse and program at the same time, and the scent of tear gas and the echoes of protests (from the Battle in Seattle to the worldwide manifestations against the invasion of Iraq) are not far from Jameson's pages at this time—remembering that this book was published in 2005, two years after the invasion of Iraq and six years after the great anti-globalization demonstrations of Seattle, Genoa, and Québec. If neoliberalism claims, in Margaret Thatcher's famous phrase, "There is no Alternative," or TINA, Jameson would have us imagine precisely this, and to "develop an anxiety about losing the future." This disruptive futurity is not invested, *à la* Lee Edelman's ferocious *No Future*, in "the usual rhetoric about 'our children'," anymore than it is in "futures" and other "derivative" investments (which we already touched on briefly in the coda to the postmodernism section), but instead is "a fear that locates the loss of the future and futuricity, of historicity itself, within the existential dimension of time and indeed within ourselves."[26]

We have seen how dialectics functions in Utopia as a veritable meme generator of critiques, which then opens up into further ramifications of the social and the future. So, critique, or the negative dialectic, or Kantian antinomies should not be misunderstood as simply a matter of affect, of leftist grumbling and dourness: they are key conceptual tools for understanding the relationship of ideology and cultural objects, and a Utopia necessarily bears some contradictory or negative relation to the social world in which it arises, or there would be no point in being Utopian, is positing a better or more attractive world. So, this is to point, first of all, to a contradiction in Utopian theory— in Jameson's conceptualization of Utopian theory—a very necessary contradiction. And he develops a metacommentary on the very necessity of such negations (Freud), or antinomies (Kant, but also Greimass), or contradictions (Marx and Hegel)—

which is to say, the value of dialectical thinking in the Utopian tradition. As we have already seen (in the discussion of his *Dog Day Afternoon* essay), Jameson is an amateur of the semiotic diagram, that structuralist form or chart or table that arranges the elements of one's analysis in a visual plane the better to understand their inner relationships; and we will offer our own version of a Greimassian semiotic rectangle in Chapter 2.

But part of how to think about negation or critique or contradiction, Jameson argues, is within the Utopian tradition itself, and here he distinguishes that tradition (he is mostly talking about science fiction) from literary modernism, in which each novel seeks to surmount all others, a clash of the titans, Proust versus Joyce, or Woolf versus Faulkner. Jameson's argument is subtle here, for his point is that the Utopian text engages with the terms of other Utopias the better to win over readers (who are really converts). This leads to the argument— to return to Jameson and our film—that the libidinal or matter of Utopian wish fulfillment in *The Wolf of Wall Street* has to do first of all with content (the oscillation between the sexual and the economic) and then form—that is, the aesthetic fore-pleasure that Freud describes.

But Jameson no doubt would not be so sanguine about this reading of a fallen document of the present age—for he also argues that the spread of global capital, and especially the sprawl of what Marx called "general intellect," signals the terminus of this kind of Utopian project. But perhaps this pessimism can be turned around—as has been argued by the various forms of Italian Marxists in the *operaismo* or Autonomists movement in the 1970s, and especially the latter day work of Hardt and Negri, Christian Marazzi, and Franco "Bifo" Berardi. With these thinkers, "immaterial labor" or Marx's "general intellect" are seen as forms of work that somehow escape from the overshadowing control of capital. I am not trying to play fast and loose with theory here—obviously stock brokers are in the service of capital—and yet there is a way to interpret the application of these workers to their task.

Work hard/play hard

There is also a very specific element of the Utopian that Jameson spends some time on in *Archaeologies of the Future* that bears great relevance to our film in question, and it has to do with the status of work. Discussing Utopian debates to be found in William Morris's *News from Nowhere* (1890) and Edward Bellamy's *Looking Backward* (1887), Jameson remarks that one key difference lies in how Bellamy's notion of labor is challenged by Morris' more aesthetic sense of a nonalienated labor. The contradiction here lies in whether a Utopia has all of us working hard, or just slacking off: which entails a more genuine freedom? Here Marx, in Volume III of *Capital*, provides the programmatic answer: "The realm of freedom really begins only where labor is determined by necessity and external expediency ends."[27] But the interesting problem lies precisely in this relationship of work to freedom, or work to leisure, which can be summed up in the phrase "work hard, play hard." *That* ideology of late capitalism is the nut to crack here: we are told, and we tell ourselves, that we work hard—we are proud of our long hours, our physical exertion or toil on the laptop.

Now, we have the Protestant work ethic rebooted: we value not just *working*, but working *hard*. And, then, that adjective, that modifier, that intensifier—"hard"—is transferred over, like an abstract condition of being—to our play, our leisure. Whether it is getting up at six in the morning on the weekend to go to a "boot camp" for fitness (or, better still, getting together with our coworkers to tackle a "Tough Mudder" or other such extreme sport) or staying up all night doing coke and cavorting with escorts—we play hard.

Here the difficulty lies for a contemporary critique of capitalism, because of how the modern day owner or "super manager" (the term is Thomas Piketty's) does, by all accounts, work hard—verified in *The Wolf of Wall Street*.[28] No longer, as the economist Michal Rozworski points out, can we on the left use those images from the 1930s of fat-cat capitalists, in top hat and spats, sitting on money bags that crush poor workers: now we need an analysis of capitalism which, instead of waving our finger in a moralistic way at the lazy rich, concentrates on how they have become, and stay, rich.

Such an imagining is what Utopias call on us to do, and at a certain point in *Archaeologies of the Future*, Jameson makes a rather concrete demand or observation:

> Few Utopian fantasies are quite so practical and potentially revolutionary in their effects as the demand for full employment, for if there is any program that could not be realized without transforming the system beyond recognition and which would at once usher in a society structurally distinct from this one in every conceivable way, from the psychological to the sociological, from the cultural to the political, it would be the demand for universal full employment in all countries of the globe, full employment at a living wage.[29]

Jameson issues a bracing challenge to the current status quo, which tells us that we need to have a certain number of people unemployed to keep wages down and profits up. But perhaps Jameson is wrong in thinking that the only function of a call for full employment would be diagnostic (although it is worth noting that Piketty has said much the same of his call for a global wealth tax, that part of its purpose would be a forensic one, to determine who owns what and where it is). The young American left thinker Benjamin Kunkel, drawing on the Keynesian economics of Michał Kalecki, agrees that full employment, with the attendant risk of inflation, but as a way to temper the boom-and-bust (or bubble-and-burst) business cycle, would not only work economically but also function as a program of "politics of the possible," *if* global full employment satisfied three criteria: actual jobs, a living wage, and guarantees from the state to step in where these are not forthcoming (through WPA-esque works programs, or support of workers' collectives).[30]

A final comment on the work of Utopia, or the Utopia of work. Jameson also remarks that a call or political program of full employment would or should attract a broad base of support: "as a resolution, it mobilizes deep-seated existential anxieties: for, despite the likelihood that most of the readers of this book are still employed, we are all of us familiar with the fear of unemployment, and not unacquainted with the psychic misery involved in chronic unemployment."[31]

Now, the political empathy on display here—for even those of us, like myself, who are employed, and specifically as a tenured academic, either will have known those other conditions in our own working life or have those close to us who have—may nonetheless be a bit generous. There are many who are remarkably clueless as to the economic conditions even of those close to them spatially or socially. But it is the specificity of "most of the readers of this book" that is crucial here: the Utopian premise that the readers and consumers and writers and participants in academic—even left academic!—conversations are themselves gainfully employed. And yet, this can no longer be assumed with any degree of good faith.

For those who work and study in the academy—in higher education—full employment is increasingly out of reach. Due to the casualization of the academic work force, the increasing reliance on underpaid adjunct labor, with little or no job security or benefits, we can no longer be surprised to realize that over 75 percent of the undergraduate teaching in US colleges and universities is carried out by nontenure-track faculty.[32] The causes are depressingly familiar: streamlining of budgets (especially at public institutions), growth of student- or customer-based programing, and the overproduction of Ph.D.s have all contributed. So, a call for full employment would do well to begin at home, in our own sector of the economy. If not, then universities and colleges will become the worst kind of enclave Utopias, sundered in more than one way from the social.

This may seem far from the concerns of this study, but let us consider how someone may be reading Jameson's book without having the well-paid job to purchase it. They may have a PDF of the book downloaded by any number of pirate or bit torrent websites: and such "victimless" crime is no doubt not only enabled by the current, postMP3 digital landscape, but can also be its own Utopian practice (think of how Pirate Bay becomes the Pirate party). And Jameson directly connects Utopian enclave fantasies in the United States to what is our topic in this film: the life of crime, going underground, living off the grid. Crime then, Jameson claims, is both a matter of opposition to the legal state, but also its own kind of collective labor.[33] So, there is a doubling of Utopian labor at work in *The Wolf of Wall Street:* first in its work hard/party hard dyad, then in its image of crime as itself nonalienated collective labor.

The enclave

One of the conundrums that Jameson faces in writing on Utopia is the simultaneity of the genre and the enclave. On the one hand, the Utopia as a literary form or genre was born at a stroke, with Thomas More's 1517 treatise—which established the convention of a Utopia being removed from the existing world, geographically in this case—on an island. And even to treat a literary Utopia as a genre is to admit to the same limitations that we find in a crime picture (or a film about Wall Street). On the other hand, the space of a Utopia is often enough "an imaginary enclave within real social space" or, even more problematically, a retreat from the dynamics of the social world. Both genre and enclave suggest a kind of fixity to the Utopian: it must fit some checklist of generic features, a conservatism of form then matched by its content. The fixity of the space or enclave means, like the Soviet experiments with communism in an actually existing capitalist world, that the enclave must always protect its features as a jealous guard against that change. Utopia first establishes or proposes a major change to the existing world (and we have already seen that this is a lamentable ontological drawback), and then allows no further changes.

The irony of the enclave may require further elaboration, which we will see in Chapter 2 when, discussing *The Wolf of Wall Street*, we discuss such spatial locations of the Utopian as general as Long Island, and as specific as an inventor's garage. Both kinds of enclaves entail a kind of retreat from the world, a retreat redolent of paranoia and other psychological effects. This is then the conundrum of Jameson's analysis— and its application in Scorsese's film—the very jubilation that attends the penny stock trader's or inventors' creation of value then leads to an anxiety that it is going to be taken away from them. So, for the viewer of a Utopian film, enjoyment is always tinged with regret. The passport you submit upon entrance to the Utopian enclave is never returned to you; you can never leave.

Jameson's examples of such Utopian enclaves are both spatial and not. In *Marxism and Form*, for instance, he offers the startling example of the Salon life as so richly described in Proust's *Recherche*. For Jameson, Proust's novel is saturated with the Utopian impulse and wish, which we can detect in Marcel's desire for his mother's kiss before bed, for a meeting with a girl, an invitation to a Salon gathering, his first trip to the theater, wishes that are at one and the same time the most infantile (or primitive) and the most sophisticated (or cultural). But it is Salon life itself, the "Proustian leisure class," which, at the very moment of its disappearance, is, Jameson claims, "not so much reactionary as anticipatory," waiting, as much of the world was when Proust was writing his novel in the 1910s and 1920s, for a different world, a world where it is not only the very rich who are free to spend their time as they wish.

The Platonic ideal for such an enclave as Utopian experiment, for Jameson, is the court, the royal household, an aristocratic center of power that is itself thought to be timeless. But he also elaborates on the enclave, or provides a combinatorial phantasmagoria, with eighteenth-century constitution drafting, royal academic societies (and even universities!), Rousseau's plans for Corsica or Poland, and modern urban planning and garden cities all vying for status in this category, for enclaves are a kind of spatial inoculation, a parasite residing in our existing world.

The dialectics of the enclave are the following: the very isolation that allows the enclave, the trench that creates the island in More, is a spatial embodiment of the ideological closure of the Utopia itself. And this closure, the spatiality of the enclave, allows for its imagination, for its ability to think of or act on a way of life, a form of society, different from and therefore a critique of the status quo; fatally, the spatiality of the enclave is both generative and a dead end. The enclave is the spatial equivalent of all of the removals from everyday life (even as Utopia is to be found in everyday life) that bedevil politics: from the Leninist Party to, arguably, the profession of politics itself (which then will necessarily trade on a demonization of its center or *locus:* hence Washington or "the Beltway" as terms of invective in America).

But this Utopian enclave is also, as a final twist of the dialectic, a sort of class or identity marker, for Jameson always betrays a fascination with Utopian thinkers as crackpots and tinkerers, who are inveterate hobbyists, for Utopianism is something anyone can come up with over the weekend, at a workbench, or in your garage. As the figure of a hobby or a workbench suggests, the notion of alienated labor still has to be clarified, which Jameson does via reference to Marx's classic writings on the matter from the Paris manuscripts: in Marx's "fourfold account," we are alienated from our tools, from the product of our labor, from productive activity (the work itself), and, finally, from species-being (our fellow or sister workers). Jameson adds a further twist, and one that speaks back to our earlier comments on leisure and "play hard," when he argues that Marx's theorization (or its realization in Utopia) has to be to read in the context of Schiller's valorization of *Spiel*, or play. And we can perhaps see that what is truly radical in *The Wolf of Wall Street* is precisely the connection between work and leisure: *here* is the Utopian-critical element.

As we have seen looking over a range of Jameson's work from the past four decades, one of the historical concerns that bedevils Marxism is its status among other critiques, rival politics—from identity politics and "new social movements" (Jameson's phrase for the 1960s) to anarchism and liberal democracy or socialism. This same problem of multiple fronts then comes to the surface in thinking about Utopia, where each program or position seems to be trapped in ideology or closure, and often disagreeing with one another to boot. Jameson's solution then (which he admits is "pluralist" but hopefully not liberal) is to acknowledge that Utopian wishes will appear, in however distorted a form, in the most ideological of projects. "Distortion" here, we now recognize, is used in its full Freudian sense, where things mean their opposite, the better to be smuggled past the border guard of our own political cowardice. We watch a movie about stockbrokers not because it tells us something about capitalism, but to see boys gone wild. And this moment of "truth" then is the *negative* notion of truth ("not because it tells us something about capitalism")— that which emerges out of its gaps and traces and paradoxes. Truth does its work and then disappears, like Weber's "vanishing mediator," or, better, the money that is smuggled to Switzerland, which material object (wrapped around a woman's body, carried in roll-on luggage), once it has been counted and tallied, is no longer of any importance. So, the Utopian truth of *The Wolf of Wall Street* lies in how it discredits Scorsese's gangster pictures for their fetish of violence; but it also shows up "finance" features for how they avoid violence.

The Wolf of Occupy

But this Utopian of the financial deserves unpacking—and will be expanded upon later—in terms of two parallel texts or events to *The Wolf of Wall Street:* the Occupy Wall Street movement (and its aftermath) and Thomas Piketty's *Capital in the Twenty-First Century*. If these are all Utopian political or cultural objects or events—the one activist, another economic-textual, the third cinematic—they offer us radically different (and yet complimentary) analysis and calls for action. Occupy Wall Street, with its strategic place/nonplace in Zuccotti Park (which is/is not the "place" of Wall Street, so already Utopian in a spatial or topological sense) and mobilization of the "99%" and critiques of debt capitalization, stands as a connection between American radical populism (which also must include the radical right of the militias in the 1990s and the Tea Party) and the international, globalized left post-Seattle (post-Arab Spring and the *indignados* in Europe).

Piketty's politicization of the economic (his *political* economy), via Big Data, mobilizes question of method (the Gini index versus distribution tables), including literary and cultural references as a way to "leaven the dough" of data mining. His work also asks us to think about justificatory rhetoric (rentier versus hypermeritocracy, the rise of the patrimonial middle class) of inequality and, in showing how inequality happens, tax regimes and choices. Thus, his breakdown of "Vautrin's lesson" from Balzac's novel *Père Goriot* shows the degree to which nineteenth-century Europe depended on inherited wealth. Finally, Piketty's call for a global tax on wealth is the most Utopian gesture imaginable, one that even David Harvey has blasted, writing that Piketty's "proposals as to the remedies for the inequalities are naïve if not utopian."[34] It is unfortunate that the left will resort to this sort of name-calling (rather parochial, one might add, as was the dickering over how much or any of Marx that Piketty had read).

Both the carnivalesque attitudes of Occupy and the cultural methodology of Piketty assure that we are right in our Jamesonian instinct to find the Utopian—but also the financial-capitalist—thread or impulse in *The Wolf of Wall Street qua* film, in its meta- or post-cinematic tropes, the voice-overs, the trans-medial incorporation of television and video, and its blatant stressing of alternate takes as if exposing the process of filmmaking (but also the process of finance capital). For it is this very critique of representation, the cornerstone or "killer app" of postmodernism, that Jameson argues comes hand-in-hand with the crisis of Utopia, with its decline as political possibility (see the discussion of how it is "easier to imagine the end of the world," above).

Here we must distinguish, Jameson argues, between the modernist crisis of representation and its postmodern aftermath. With modern film—say, Kurosawa or Hitchcock—the bewildering array of relative P.O.V.s in *Rashomon* (1950) or sudden discovery of female duplicity in *Vertigo* (1958) instantiate "heroic formal invention" on the part of the *auteurs*. But the narrative layers in *The Matrix* (Andy Wachowski, Lana Wachowski, 1999) or *Inception* do something altogether different: for with postmodernism the question of referentiality or representation is no longer as it was for the moderns a problem; instead, it is sidestepped, and we have the fragmentation of narratives, images, and leading characters. As we have seen and will further explore with respect to *The Wolf of Wall Street*, the "reflexivity" of its meta-cinematic tropes—the way they reflect their very formation as images, the color of a car, another car's narrative of successful or unsuccessful driving—demands a similar reflexivity of Utopia and, I will argue, of a critique of finance capitalism and its claims to represent industrial economics.

But Jameson also does not want us to fall for the postmodern "cynical reason" valorized by these multiple images (they are all lying) and seeks as well to determine what kind of political project can grab hold of our imagination—after moving through various social histories (including Ferdinand Braudel on the Mediterranean) he discusses the more recent political experiments of federalism, which have met with some recent setbacks in Spain and Canada as separatist movements have asserted the logic of differentiation (or micro-nationalism). But the federation lacks representation, or reference, for political reasons similar to the cinematic ones discussed above. The Utopian project needs some point of identification—or even fetish—the better to garner support, and yet, Jameson avers, this does not seem likely.

By way of concluding this discussion of Jameson and Utopia, I want to wrench that adjective or noun (Utopian, Utopia) out of the hands of the neoliberal pragmatists for whom "Utopian" inevitably means unworkable or pie-in-the-sky (or even dangerous). First of all, we have to declare that it is rather neoliberalism, or capitalism, that is the most Utopian of all ideologies, with its belief in unfettered progress and growth, a belief that depends not only on the unequal exploitation of labor and workers both in the (over) developed world and on a global scale of gross inequity, but also on a shortsightedness with respect to the ecological state of the planet, from depleted oceans and peak oil/tar sands/fracking atrocities to such (literal) canaries in the mine as pesticide and monocultural genome seeds and their effects on insect, bee, and avian populations.

The belief that we can continue to consume our smartphones and skinny jeans and frappuccinos in the face of Foxconn worker suicides and mega city slum explosions and imperial war mongering is what is Utopian. And here a meme in the Jameson-Žižek conversation is worth considering, beginning with Jameson's assertion in *Archeologies of the Future:* "[i]f it is so, as someone has observed, that it is easier to imagine the end of the world than the end of capitalism, we probably need another term to characterize the increasingly popular visions of total destruction and of the extinction of life on Earth." The story of this meme has been ably documented on the *Qlipoth* blog, but a short version is that the phrase first appears in Jameson's essay "The Antinomies of Postmodernity," when he admits that "[i]t seems easier for us to imagine the thoroughgoing deterioration of the earth and of nature than the breakdown of late capitalism; perhaps that is due to some weakness of our imaginations." Žižek in turn cites Jameson— "it seems easier to imagine the 'end of the world' than a far more modest change in the mode of production" and at a certain point the meme continues in Jameson's other writings (including the "Future City" essay), in the *Žižek!* documentary and his speech at Occupy Wall Street, and no doubt into the future. It may be easier to imagine the destruction of the planet than the end of this particular meme … [35]

But this frustrated or stymied Utopian wish, it turns out, is fundamental, Jameson argues, to "the desire called Utopia" (from the subtitle to *Archaeologies*). The reader will be unsurprised that he expresses this in a dialectical fashion: Utopian affect is to be found in the production of an "unresolvable contradiction" (which Jameson calls an aesthetic project), even as such lack of resolution allows for the persistence of the Utopian wish.

Utopia: Coda

For the past few years, Jameson has been giving a talk on "An American Utopia," in which he offers up the specter of a complete militarization of American society—but as a Utopian proposition, mischievously referencing a 1950s cartoon in which Eisenhower remarks that if one wants universal health care, one need only do as he did, and join the Army. This talk is being published in a forthcoming collection that will include responses by Kathi Weeks, Alberto Toscano, Jodi Dean, Michael Hardt, among others. For Jameson, militarization would be a form of dual power, a second government alongside representative democracy that is neither space-bound (as in the Utopian enclave) nor time-constrained (as in an uprising of the Occupy Wall Street or Arab Spring varieties).

This universalism, accompanied by a pedagogical disciplinary effect much admired by Trotsky, Jameson argues, would then create the conditions for a Utopia which neither underestimates the power of envy (what Lacan and Žižek call, he reminds us, the "theft of enjoyment") nor forbids, amazingly, the very subject matter of our film, the stock market and its entrepreneurialism, the former meaning that "some new form of production or value competition needs to be invented here," the latter a recognition of the creativity embodied in the entrepreneur, whether that figure be the older idea of an inventor (Thomas Edison, Henry Ford) or the more recent one of the designer (Steve Jobs).[36] This new foray into "thinking the impossible" on the part of Jameson is a useful reminder that it is possible for the left to have a critique of finance capital not mired in moralizing; we will see how Utopian a film it is that we are discussing here in the following chapter.

Critical reception

Before turning to our film, it is important to give due consideration to some of the critical response that Jameson's work has elicited over the past four decades. Evidently, this is a large archive all in itself: even in 1982, upon the publication of *The Political Unconscious*, the then-influential journal *diacritics* devoted an entire issue to that book, and there have been at least seven book-length studies including five monographs (by William C. Dowling, Steven Helmling, Sean Homer, Adam Roberts, and myself) and two collections of essays. Then, in 2009, following a conference on the twenty-fifth anniversary of *The Political Unconscious*, the journal *Representations* presented an issue on critiques of Jamesonian or "symptomatic" readings in favor of "surface" or "cognitive" interpretations. And there have been many interventions and engagements with his film criticism and his writings on postmodernism. A selective overview might note the following: first, the ways in which critiques of symptomatic criticism have been confined, in a very *un*-Jamesonian way, to literary criticism (and, not surprisingly, have denied the notion of the unconscious as a way of not attending to the endgame of literary scholarship); engagements with Jameson's film criticism locate it in the broader spectrum of political (but also *Screen*) film theory, which itself has come under attack or closure since the 1990s (the so-called "post-theory" debate); finally, the local critiques of Jameson's work on postmodernism in the 1980s focused (here I am thinking of the interventions by

Eagleton, Davis, and Silliman) on the need for a more engaged and politicized notion of postmodern culture.

Surface and symptom

To take these bodies of critique in that order, then, the construction of a "surface reading" that stands as a new, retooled (or rebooted) successor to symptomatic reading (call it Symptomatic 2.0 or perhaps the symptomatic after a hostile takeover) is announced in the introduction to the issue of *Representations* mentioned above, by Stephen Best and Sharon Marcus. There are many valences to Best and Marcus's overview of the new interpretive paradigms—they range in their text over questions of the unconscious, of attentiveness, of surface as materiality or the verbal or ethics—but for our purposes here the most compelling, because historicizing, argument is that, simply, we critics don't need such fancy interpretive paradigms, because it's so obvious how bad things are now:

> The assumption that domination can only do its work when veiled, which may once have sounded almost paranoid, now has a nostalgic, even utopian ring to it. Those of us who cut our intellectual teeth on deconstruction, ideology critique, and the hermeneutics of suspicion have often found those demystifying protocols superfluous in an era when images of torture at Abu Ghraib and elsewhere were immediately circulated on the internet…and many people instantly recognized as lies political statements such as "mission accomplished.[37]

Best and Marcus are both right and wrong here, it seems to me: right to attempt to locate their interpretive shift in the present moment of post-9/11 hegemony, but wrong to think that one should therefore abandon symptomatic criticism. Two objections can be made to this move on their part: first, that to understand the images of Abu Ghraib, for instance, is not necessarily a project without its own challenges (to work through the context of the US occupation of Iraq, the gender and racial politics of the American prison and guards, the photographic process that sees the taking of pictures as a form of harassment or torture, the digital and internet politics of those pictures' dissemination, censorship, and ensuing moral panic)—this might very well be a cultural object or event that calls for the very broadening of semantic (and image) horizons that Jameson calls for in *The Political Unconscious*.[38] But it is this very illusion that what is at the surface of a text should be obvious—and therefore not delved into—that Jameson identifies as the "hermeneutic paradox" in *Archaeologies of the Future*, where he considers how a critic, looking for a hidden Utopian impulse, then reads an explicitly Utopian text. And this is our challenge in discussing *The Wolf of Wall Street*, to determine what *is* the surface, what *is* the subtext—and, perhaps, whether those metaphors are still of use.

But there may be other reasons for the distaste some today have with Jamesonian readings (leaving aside the Oedipal resonance of Best and Marcus's claim that they "cut [their] intellectual teeth on deconstruction, ideology critique, and the hermeneutics of suspicion"). In a trenchant takedown of surface reading, Carolyn Lesjak aligns the practice with a "Third Way" form of neoliberalism, where the humble critic is content to lower one's expectations in the face of the luminous truth of the text, an attack on theory concomitant with the crisis in the humanities, but also, she argues, helps us to think of a form of critical practice that emerges out of the gap *between* the Marxist, or symptomatic, reading, and a surface reading.[39] But this strategy no doubt has a pragmatic valence, one of neoliberal academia that wants to "move on" from the distasteful politics of the past, whether conceived of in terms of decades—the 1960s or the 1990s—or threats to the professoriat—identity politics—or matters of dubious affect— again, for example, paranoia.

I close this engagement with surface reading by noting another form in which the critiques take place, or at least its metaphorical associations. In Mary Thomas Crane's "cognitive reading" of Jameson's *The Political Unconscious*,[40] she particularly notes how Jameson's technique calls for a "violent intervention" that results in grotesque imagery: "Readers who perform the semantic reconstruction of key terms are able to retrieve 'a whole historical ideology that must be drawn, massy and dripping, up into the light before the text can be considered to be read'," an image at one with one of my favorites from *The Political Unconscious*, when Jameson declares that "[o]nly Marxism can give us an adequate account of the essential mystery of the cultural past, which, like Tiresias drinking the blood, is momentarily returned to life and warmth and allowed once more to speak, and to deliver its long-forgotten message in surroundings utterly alien to it."[41] But Jameson's "alien" here may be a clue to what really disturbs Crane, for this is something like the monster in *Alien* that Jameson is bringing to the surface, the monster that is the Real of history, and that surface reading would prefer not to inquire into too deeply. Or, to stay with a film that Jameson discusses, consider how David Cronenberg's *Videodrome* enacts a grisly insertion/extraction of precisely such "massy and dripping" objects as videotapes and guns into and out of a vaginal slot in James Wood's stomach (which imagery, Jameson argues, is not gendered but instead signals our anxieties about who is doing what to whom in late capitalism). There objects which are also ideological (or ideologemes: the now superseded video cassette, the still relevant automatic pistol) denote as well a horror with the cultural which does not seem to be too far off from the horror with symptomatic readings. Jameson argues with respect to *Videodrome* and which may stand as a rebuke to surface reading even as it helps us to think about *The Wolf of Wall Street*, that film is simultaneously about the economic, the sexual, the social, politics, morality. Even the surface turns out to have depth, as David Hockney said, and so thematics recombine themselves in an endless shell game. And to remind us that perhaps the partisans of surface reading are too much caught up in their disciplinary hang-ups as literary critics, Jameson locates in *Videodrome* the place where words are themselves just images, media junk (the film, concerning a porn channel and videos that brainwash their viewers, features a Marshall McLuhan-type media prophet)—which border-blur is also to be seen in the trans-mediality of *The Wolf of Wall Street*. If both Scorsese and Cronenberg's films feature key moments of the interruption of film by video or television, it is Jameson's critique that can bring such ideological interventions to light.

The Post-theory challenge

We have perhaps taken too long describing what may be an internecine battle in the dusty pages of literary scholarship, and it is time to look at how Jameson's writing on film has been received in contemporary film scholarship. But this is no easy matter, as the very prominence of Jameson as a figure means that he must be acknowledged (and so even an anti-theory enterprise like Bordwell and Carroll's *Post-Theory* devotes an entire chapter to his work) but then he will be misread in, well, fairly *symptomatic* ways that take him to task for not doing what his work does not set out to do, that refuse in turn to engage with his premises (the role of allegory, or periodization). Bill Nichols, however, in a thorough and evenhanded account of "the formalism wars," is particularly astute when he sets Bordwell off against Jameson, noting the ways in which Bordwell focuses on the coherence of a film not only internally (narrative, the use of formal devices such as shots and lighting) but *qua* film, as though "cinema had remained thematically, formally, and institutionally immune to television and commerce," a diametrically different approach to understanding film than we have seen in the "trans-medial" readings of Jameson.[42]

It is therefore worth examining a more thorough engagement with Jameson's film writings: Michael Walsh's chapter on

Jameson in *Post-Theory*. Walsh's argument is rather one of pulling back the curtain: Jameson, he tells us, "is openly Hegelian," by which Walsh means Jameson is "more interested in the Visual than in visual detail."[43] For Walsh, the scope of Jameson's historical categories, the range of his filmic references, and his critique of the empirical fallacy mean that, as the theme of *Post-Theory* will have it, "many of the problems of film theory have been caused by generalizing from ideas that seem to have suggestive power" (494). Thus, Walsh will argue that Jameson's account of the conspiracy film is not sufficiently precise in its imputing a postmodern or late capitalist cause to the narratives in, say, *The Parallax View* or *Videodrome*, but as I have argued, it is the specificity of Jameson's critical intervention into the characters and object worlds of these films—the pathological or Real—that anchors his film criticism.

Along with Lesjak's account of the surface reading critique (where she also cites *Post-Theory*, bringing it to task for its disingenuously modest self-description as "middle-level theories"), the most persuasive account of this debate may be Matthew Flisfeder's. He reminds us of Jameson's distinction, in *The Political Unconscious*, between subjective and objective modes of cultural criticism, the first denoting the workings of ideology and the second the material basis of the film. Proponents of *Post-Theory*, Flisfeder remarks, believe themselves to be in scholarly pursuit of "objective, neutral knowledge towards its object," while Jameson and other figures of disparagement freely acknowledge (as we saw in my discussion of *The Political Unconscious*) their own investment in the subjective.[44] Walsh gets it exactly wrong, for instance, when he quibbles over whether nostalgia films are a genre, for Jameson is not a librarian or a stockboy applying labels to DVD cases.

By way of a final comment on recent critiques of Jameson's work (attacks on "symptomatic readings" in literary scholarship and on theory in film studies), I want to return briefly to the example I gave earlier of an allegorical interpretation: the scene from Hitchcock's *Rear Window*. Now, this argument was a bit of a cheat or a lure: a cheat that allowed me to ventriloquize Jameson on Hitchcock, but also a lure because the debate between Jeff and Lisa/Tom is also a debate over surface and symptomatic readings—but in a film. Lisa and Tom's counterarguments to Jeff's claim that a murder took place are that, first, it is morbid to watch people; second, no one would murder someone in full view of others; and third, he did not actually see the killing or the body. The first, moral, critique then is similar to surface readers' claims that symptomatic interpretations are paranoid. The second and third contradict each other and thus end up supporting Jeff's (and Jameson's) symptomatic critique. But the banter should not lead us to ignore what is also an economic subcurrent in the film itself. As Tania Modleski points out, the gender politics between Jeff and Lisa are not simply a matter of the male gaze and female passivity (since Jeff is laid up with his broken leg, Lisa is the one who actually visits the apartment in question).[45] Early in the film, Lisa models a dress she is wearing, which costs, she tells Jeff, $1,100. Surprised, eyebrows lifted, he asks if it is listed on the stock exchange. An opponent of symptomatic readings, it turns out, is heavily "invested" in financial capital, which interpretation requires, to no great surprise, a willingness to look beneath the surface. This will be the project of the next chapter.

CHAPTER TWO

How to Watch *The Wolf of Wall Street*

Introduction

The Wolf of Wall Street's ambivalent take on Wall Street is of a piece with Scorsese's *oeuvre* (situated by way of comparison with *Mean Streets*, *The King of Comedy* [1982], and *Goodfellas*), but also helps us to think about the vicissitudes of finance capital itself, for the plot of the film can be related dialectically to the Marxist theory of crisis. Following the lead of Jameson's essay on *Dog Day Afternoon*, I examine the role of class in the film, finding it figured, first, in the collectivity of Belfort's sales team, the "crew" he assembles like a robbery gang, but also in the film's presentation of Stratton Oakmont in opposition to the Wall Street establishment, a presentation that even offers a lesson on the subprime mortgage run that precipitated the 2008 economic crisis. Jameson's theory of postmodernism then offers a rubric by which to examine especially the media volatilization on offer in the film—its juxtaposition of TV and film is particularly crucial here—as well as more common Scorsese tics and moments of self-reflexivity. A politics of the film, of its unconscious, then can be determined in terms of its *non-dit*, its unsaid, or at least its propensity for rudely ejecting or killing off characters in a fairly symptomatic fashion. But I finally make an argument for viewing *The Wolf of Wall Street* as a Utopian film, not only in the ontological sense stressed by Bloch (as a work of art), but also in terms of its most unattractive features, its misogyny and treatment of small people, as well as its more conventional spatialization of the Utopian, via the enclave (although here, again, with the film's description of the "Guinea Gulch" and the "Guinea gangplank," we may find something to object to).

The dialectics of the film

Jameson's approach to film is dialectical, which means two things. First, he looks at individual films in relation to the social world, to history, to the political. Second, he works out that relation in terms of a film's formal components. So, what does this mean when we come to a film like *The Wolf of Wall Street?* Two contradictory propositions come to mind. The first is that the film is a celebration of Wall Street, of the stockbroker lifestyle: fast cars, big houses, hookers, and blow. Who wouldn't want that? The second is the opposite proposition: the film shows how stupid Jordan Belfort and his crew are, how excessive their pleasures, and punishes them for that excess. And, as any fan of Martin Scorsese knows all too well, this kind of nuanced approach is very much his style: time and again his heroes run up against the results of their untamed id, their American desires. This kind of nuance may actually be characteristic of Hollywood film, of commercial film, in general, driven as it is by test screenings, focus groups, and the desire to sell as many tickets at possible. Nonetheless, to return to the specifics of *The Wolf of Wall Street*, perhaps that nuance, that dialectic, can be located historically (as Jameson always wants us to do) in terms of the history of finance capital itself, the 500-year history of stock markets and bubbles and investing that began in Europe in the early 1600s. Because a Jamesonian interpretation would want us not merely to find the social history reflected in the content of the film, but also in its form, perhaps the very form, or in this case plot, of the film is the same boom and bust, exuberance and crisis, of the stock market.

Beyond ethics

As noted earlier, when I described this book project to friends, a common reaction to the notion of using Marxist theory to talk about a film about Wall Street was—Of course! The book must write itself! But the obvious nature of this insight—a film about Wall Street is going to be a political film—does not mean we should neglect it. We should not neglect this insight because it is actually complicated.

So, is *The Wolf of Wall Street* pro or con finance capitalism? And yet, even to phrase the question in this way is to suggest that it is one or the other. The film is pro Wall Street because it shows how much fun the stockbrokers have: Jordan Belfort has a fast car, a big house, a beautiful wife. His friends have snappy suits, make millions, indulge in all kinds of drugs and casual sex, and, even, seem to enjoy their work. What's not to like?

But the contrary position immediately suggests itself, doesn't it? Not only are these superficial pleasures—and many of them are illegal (cocaine, prostitution), or unethical (dwarf-tossing, humiliating a worker by shaving her head)—but they are also the rewards for what the film depicts as dubious, if not, again, illegal, stock broking. Belfort and his crew start out selling penny stocks, or stocks in companies too small to be listed on NASDAQ—selling these penny stocks to working-class and lower-middle class "schmucks." Typical clients are postmen and plumbers, Belfort is told when he first visits the boiler room operation, "they see our ads in the back of *Hustler, Popular Mechanics* and they actually say they can get rich quick."

There is also a forlorn tawdriness to Belfort's pleasures. As Bloch remarks, "All criminals, even if they come from the scum of the earth, are petit-bourgeois, the good life is only possible in affluence, that is what they want."[1] This may be a place where *Goodfellas* meets *The Godfather*: the "scum of the earth" criminal wishes to ascend to the petit bourgeois status of Don Corleone. But then *The Wolf of Wall Street* inhabits a revolving door of cinematic ontology *qua* genre—is it a crime film pretending to be a Wall Street film, or the other way around, or is there really any difference (in which case, Bloch's quip applies to all of Scorsese)?

And yet, even the list of "superficial" pleasures should not be underestimated. Or, rather, its dismissal is perhaps too moralistic, the finger-waving we expect from political or Marxist criticism. So, let us go a bit deeper, for what dialectical criticism entails is not so much a matter of positive or negative images of a given activity. Questions such as "does the film make selling penny stocks look like fun?" or "are the characters properly punished for their nefarious deeds?" treat filmgoing as an ethics class, and ignore how film itself works. A more nuanced way to think about the question of the film's politics with respect to finance capital would be to ask with whom the film encourages us to identify—do we identify with Belfort and his crew? Do we identify with the humiliated dwarf or the employee whose head is shaved? Do we identify with the prostitutes or with Belfort's clients (most of whom, we never see?). These questions answer themselves, arguably: we identify with Belfort and his buddies: with Azoff, but also perhaps with his wife?

So, now we have a set of questions or propositions about how the film treats finance capital, how it depicts the "masters of the universe," or stockbrokers: how it treats the pleasures that are a reward for the rich; how it depicts the stockbroking activity itself—the dynamics of finance capital; how it encourages the viewer to identify with various characters in the film, the—let us be crude here—winners and the losers. A look at two scenes in the film may help us in this regard: a scene where Belfort is cavorting with a prostitute, and the scene where he first learns how to sell stocks.

The first scene takes place during the film's set up, when Belfort, via voice-over, is telling us about his various luxury possessions, including his "mansion, private jet, yacht, six cars, two vacation homes," and his wife, a former Miller Lite model: visuals include a *Lifestyles of the Rich and Famous* montage of said yacht and its staff, Naomi in lingerie. Then Belfort adds, he also gambles "like a degenerate," drinks "like a fish," has sex with prostitutes five or six times a week, has "three federal agencies looking to indict" him, and "loves drugs." This is an odd list of habits for Belfort to cop to at the start of the film. He takes a sad pride in those habits, surely. And why mention the federal agencies? Is flouting the law another bad habit—is Belfort addicted to going to the edge of being arrested for his malfeasance?

Belfort's litany of habits takes place as the film shifts from the montage of luxury and fantasy items to a quick scene, less than a minute, showing Belfort snorting cocaine off the body of a prostitute. As he declares, in the voice-over, that he loves drugs, Belfort jerks his head up from that very drug-taking, and looks around anxiously as if suddenly aware that he is being watched. This is a very meta-moment that mixes a certain realism (coke-induced paranoia) with cinematic reflexivity (is he being watched by the moviegoer, or by the FBI?). And it also indicates, I argue, a high degree of ambiguity on the part of the film: to be sure, Belfort is living a luxurious lifestyle, but equally certain is that such pleasures are hollow indeed.

The other illustration of the film's dialectics comes when Belfort learns how to sell stocks. But here I mean to compare two scenes, or two scene sequences. The first is well known: Mark Hanna (Matthew McConaughey), Belfort's first boss at the high-end firm L.F. Rothschild, takes him out for lunch, the archetypal "three martini lunch." The second scene is perhaps more obscure: when Belfort, having lost his job at the prestigious firm, is reduced to selling penny stocks in Long Island. The first scene is a bravura performance on the part of McConaughey: not only does Hanna advise Belfort to drink copiously, do coke, and masturbate to keep up his sales performance, but he also finishes by thumping his chest in a bizarre primate ritual, humming along, getting Belfort to join in. Selling stocks is an obscene endeavor, but also kind of fun.

Soon enough, however, Belfort, loses that job after the Black Monday stock market crash of 1987; following a newspaper ad, he visits the Investor Center in a Long Island strip plaza. After one of the brokers, Dwayne, explains how the system works, Belfort gets onto the phone and we see his technique—really, he is genius—at work, as he convinces a client to invest $4,000. Unlike his former job selling "blue-chip" or respectable stocks, for which Belfort made a 1 percent commission, here he makes 50 percent. Belfort tells us in a voice-over: "I was selling garbage to garbage men, and making cash hand over fist." Sound and visual aspects of this scene underscore the downmarket place from which Belfort builds his fortune. When his wife Teresa points out the job ad to him, he reads out, "Stockbrokers, Long Island? Stockbrokers in Long Island." The repetition signals Belfort's disbelief that a real job was to be had in the outer boroughs. He drives up to the plaza, and we see a shot of Belfort from inside the brokerage, through a filthy glass door. A toilet flushes, and a man emerges from the washroom at the back, zipping his fly. This is not a posh Manhattan firm.

But comparing these two scenes is not merely a matter of showing how far Belfort has dropped: rather, what is apparent are the continuities between these two accounts of the ethics of finance capital. Whether it is a matter of getting coked up to make sales of blue-chip stocks or ripping off working-class schmucks to sell them worthless paper, a matter of chest thumping or grimy windows, stockbroking is a filthy business. This is a different conclusion from the one reached just now about how we are to view Belfort's sex and drugs lifestyle: one an ambiguous portrayal of that lifestyle, the other two different portrayals with a similar thesis. Dialectics is not a matter of a "balanced" or two-sided approach to a question: it is not "bipartisanship" as a form of film criticism.

Scorsese's bad boys

But let us follow up this idea of nuance, let us continue to entertain the proposition that *The Wolf of Wall Street* encourages neither a moralistic dismissal of the stock broker nor a simple-minded emulation of that lifestyle. Perhaps this is true of much of the Scorsese filmography. It is almost a cliché of writing on Scorsese for critics to find either an apology for masculine brutality or an exploration of the limits of his characters' overcompensation. If we look at Scorsese's gangster films, *Mean Streets*, *Goodfellas*, *Casino* (1995), and *Departed* (2006), the heroes are sympathetically portrayed even as their actions lead to dire consequences. Thus, Charlie (Harvey Keitel), the sensitive hood in *Mean Streets*, tries to reconcile the demands of the Mafia soldier's life with loyalty to his psychotic friend Johnny Boy (Robert de Niro); while, in *Goodfellas*, Henry Hill (Ray Liotta) and Jimmy Conway (de Niro) have to cover for their (again) psychotic buddy Tommy deVito (Joe Pesci).

Are we to view Charlie and Henry as men who stick by their friends even when it is unpopular (or suicidal, given their organized crime milieu)? Or are they idiots, saps, who make the wrong choices again and again? The films do not make it easy for us to make that determination, in part because of how they invite us to identify with the heroes. In the case of *Mean Streets*, which Scorsese has claimed to be an autobiographical film, Charlie is a sympathetic character whose ethical dilemma viewers will identify with even as they do not wish to be a low-level *Mafiosi*. His actions are alternatively positive and negative. He is loyal to his friend Johnny, he ignores prejudicial attitudes toward his epileptic girlfriend Teresa, and he has a strong religious bent. However, Charlie only wishes to advance in a Mafia *milieu* by taking over a restaurant whose owner owes money to Charlie's uncle; he is given to sexist and racist outbursts; and his ethics clash with what may well be a self-satisfied, preening, ego.

A similar dialectic can be seen in *Goodfellas*, where Henry's success in the lower echelons of the Mafia ensures a degree of material comfort. The nuance here is developed in a different way than in *Mean Streets* for, based as *Goodfellas* is on Nicholas Pileggi's memoir, it offers a "thick" description of the crime lifestyle. As with *Mean Streets*, *Goodfellas* is concerned with working-class criminals, not the CEOs that we find in *The Godfather*. Henry's success is relative: yes, we see him in a good suit, or, in a famous tracking shot, skipping the line at a restaurant. But even that luxury (coming in through the Copacabana's basement kitchen) is a small pleasure, and Henry has to shell out many $20 bills along the way, as his girlfriend Karen notes. So, the dialectical nuance here lies in how Henry's luxury is circumscribed by his place in the Mafia hierarchy—most notably, when he turns to drug dealing over his *capo* Paulie's objections later in the film, which leads to Henry's downfall.

But the split interpretations that these two films offer us can be seen most clearly, I think, with two parallel bar fight scenes. *Mean Streets* is full of bar fights—coupled with his use of doo-wop and girl group music, the tussles are veritable musical dance sequences. But the climactic scene, where the loan shark Michael confronts Johnny Boy over his nonpayment of a debt, is crucial for how it tests our willingness to approve of Charlie. Johnny has been avoiding Michael—he owes him $3,000 and is also in debt to other neighborhood lenders—and the film has portrayed Michael's persistence itself in ambiguous ways. Michael is both a figure of doom, who threatens he will break both of Johnny's legs, and a maladroit wannabe, who intrudes onto an earlier scene between Charlie and his uncle. So, when Michael comes into the bar to demand payment of his loan, the show-down promises both action and its frustration. Michael asks for his money, Johnny gives him ten dollars—an insult—and after Michael rejects such a pittance, they tussle, with Johnny pulling a gun that we have already seen him use. Michael leaves, Charlie remonstrates with Johnny, and decides they'd better leave. After picking up Teresa, they drive to Brooklyn, where the trio is gunned down by Michael and his henchman Shorty (played by Scorsese).

A similar scene takes place in *Goodfellas*, when Tommy (Joe Pesci), tired of being called a "shoeshine boy" by returned-from-prison Billy Batts (Frank Vincent), stabs and then shoots Batts. The scene is played for more tension: we soon learn that Batts is a "made man" in the Mafia hierarchy. The scene escalates with Batts insulting Tommy, who answers back, but is immediately covered for by Henry. In effect, this is the same logic as in *Mean Streets*: the hero (Charlie or Henry) has to keep apologizing to a Mafia figure (Michael or Billy) for the words and actions of the hero's friend (Johnny or Tommy). There is a difference in terms of how it all plays out; in *Goodfellas*, Tommy kills Batts (with some help from Jimmy), followed by the disposal of Batts' body, with a digression for dinner at Tommy's mother's house. But this is an unauthorized killing (the internecine logic of Mafia hierarchies is that Tommy, not a made man, cannot kill a *Mafiosi* without permission), and, later in the film, we learn of Tommy's own demise. So, in effect, *Goodfellas* depicts a more intricate chain of command, whereas *Mean Streets* has a more direct cause-and-effect narrative logic; but in both cases, I would argue that, like Charlie or Henry, we cannot decide where our loyalties should be.

And we can also test this theory—that a Scorsese film will often present us with a hero who is both likable and problematic—with its counterargument. Thus, in *The King of Comedy*, perhaps the problem is that the film is *not* nuanced enough in its portrayal of the fan as stalker. That film begins with the frenzy of fandom—the *melée* that surrounds talk show host Jerry Langford (Jerry Lewis) when he leaves his studio. Jerry is surrounded by autograph hounds and can barely make it to his limo. When he gets inside the car, Masha (Sandra Bernhard) attacks him, but Jerry escapes, the shot freezing on Masha's hand on the car window as the credits roll. But this opening ambivalence is hardly borne out by the film's story. True, the film portrays the manic lunacy of Masha and Rupert Pupkin (Robert de Niro) as they stalk and eventually kidnap Jerry. However, in the end, Rupert does his comedy bit on Jerry's show and after a prison term, becomes a veritable king of comedy. Or does he? For what is dialectical about *The King of Comedy* may lie in its use of fantasy sequences. Three or four times in the film we see Rupert in conversation on Jerry's talk show, shown to be a matter of Rupert's delusions when he is brought out of his reverie by his screeching mother's voice (played by Scorsese's own mother). A similar use of fantasy, I will argue, underwrites *The Wolf of Wall Street*'s dialectics.

The stock market

A dialectical theory of film is not only a matter of proposing different possible interpretations of the film: dialectics is also, in Marxist theory, a matter of connecting that film itself to a historical context. In the case of *The Wolf of Wall Street*, dialectics requires of us that we relate its story to the history of finance capital itself, to the stock market not merely as an instrument for raising capital for companies, but in terms of the stock market's role in society at large. That history goes back to the trading of shares in the Dutch East India Company at the Amsterdam Stock Exchange, beginning in 1602; but for our purposes we can concentrate on the period covered by the film, from immediately prior to the 1987 crash to its post-Occupy present. Here two approaches suggest themselves: first, the portrayal of stock market mechanisms: how accurately does the film depict the penny stocks sales and IPOs (Initial Public Offerings) that were the object of Belfort's business? Second, the relationship between the film and the recent history of finance capitalism: in what way does the film reflect the post-1990s market?

The Wolf of Wall Street presents us with three stages in its depiction of finance capital: the pre-1987 glory years of Wall Street—when Belfort briefly works at a legit firm and is educated by Mark Hanna on the dubious nature of finance; the selling of penny stocks, both for its own sake and after luring investors with blue chips; and using insider trading of IPOs to drive up stock prices. Belfort's first day at work sees him arrive at an open plan office (identified as L.F. Rothschilds), where he is immediately thrown into an obscene maelstrom. His first supervisor tells him he is "pond scum," Hanna congratulates him for pitching a stock during his job interview, and, as the market opens with a bell and brokers start calling clients, Belfort asks us, "You want to know what money sounds like? Go to a trading floor on Wall Street." Letting off a string of profanities, Belfort continues, "I couldn't believe how these guys talked to each other. I was hooked in seconds, it was like mainlining adrenaline."

Hanna makes his first sale of the day—remarkably, a 2,000 share order for Microsoft—and dispatches the paperwork via pneumatic tube. The cacophony of the trading floor is replaced by a syncopated drumming: cut to Belfort sitting in a restaurant, nonplussed, as Hanna thumps his chest. This scene we have already visited, to stress the obscenity of Belfort's training. But equally important is when Hanna passes on a trade secret. Nobody, Hanna admits, knows how a stock is going to do. "It's all a *fugazi*," he says, using the Italian term for "fake" to describe the nature of stockbroker's work. "We don't create shit, we don't build anything," and so the broker's purpose is to make sure his clients keep reinvesting any profits from stocks, thereby earning more commission for the broker.

But Belfort really starts making money after Black Monday, when he gets into the penny stock game with the Long Island boiler room operation. Here, as he gleefully admits, he was "selling garbage to garbage men," or cheap stocks to working-class people, but Belfort soon has a Damascene moment, a conversion of sorts. He presents a piece of jewelry to his wife Teresa, who asks him if he wouldn't feel better selling his stocks to rich people, who could afford to lose money. Rich people don't buy penny stocks, he tells her, because they are too smart. They are too smart to buy stocks from people like his crew, the Long Island schmucks he has assembled to flog penny stocks.

So, Belfort decides to "reinvent the company," gives Stratton Oakmont a regal logo, and tells his salesmen that they are going to start targeting the "1 percent," adding, "I'm talking about whales here, Moby-fucking-Dick," using a script for telephone sales that he has written, which, continuing the *Moby-Dick* metaphor, he says is their "harpoon," with which he will teach them to be "Captain fucking Ahab." "Captain who?" a character asks, and Belfort is thrown by this—for you can be certain that Melville's novel is not on anybody's bedside table.

Nevertheless, Belfort's crew is soon very proficient at a key task: selling blue-chip stocks to the "1 percent," and using said sales as "bait" with which to then sell penny stocks. But even this level of profit (remember, penny stocks had a commission of 50 percent) is not enough, and we then have a third form of stock larceny: insider trading. The climactic scene for this monumental profit-taking occurs when Stratton Oakmont gets the highly coveted IPO for Steve Madden shoes, a trendy New York fashion house. At two moments, midpoint through the film, Belfort is explaining to the camera how IPOs work:

> An IPO is an initial public offering. It is the first time a stock is offered for sale to the general population. Now, as the firm taking the company public, we set the initial sales price then sold those shares right back to our friends. Yet ... look, I know you're not following what I'm saying anyway, right? That's okay, that doesn't matter. (*Whispering*) The only question was this, was all this legal? Absolutely fucking not. But we were making more money than we knew what to do with. And what do you do when you're making more money than you know what to do with?

Cut to stacks of money in safety deposit boxes, a huge ring for Naomi.

Twenty minutes later in the film, Stratton Oakmont is engaged in its largest IPO ever, for Steve Madden shoes, and again Belfort addresses the camera: "Of the two million shares offered for sale, a million belonged to me, held in phony accounts held by my ratholes. Now, once the price hit the high teens...(Laughs) You know what, who gives a shit? As always, the point is this"—and we see Azoff pop champagne, screaming "22 million dollars in three fucking hours!"

To summarize the film's three lessons in the stock market: we have a market that is manifestly about fakery, to which one's only rational response is drugs, alcohol, and masturbation. When that doesn't work, one relies on metaphors from American literature to hook the 1 percent. And to make even more money—well, the film says, who cares, it's illegal, and we did it.

So, how does this accord with Wall Street as such, the historical entity that was finance capitalism in the late twentieth century? Here two problems come immediately to mind: first, the film depicts a subculture of stock brokerages on the margins of the industry. "Boiler room" or "bucket shop" operations like Stratton Oakmont generally sell to inexperienced investors, trying to stuff their portfolios with worthless stocks. They are not the "white shoe" or prestigious brokerages and investment bankers, like Rothschilds, where Belfort begins his career. So, there is a class relationship being explored in the film, crucial to understanding why Belfort, when he is making his firm more upscale, tells his brokers that Stratton Oakmont appeared to be so old that its founders came over on *The Mayflower*. This class dynamic is evident in a scene between Belfort and the FBI agent, when Belfort claims he could pass on information about more established Wall Street firms like Goldman Sachs, the Lehman Brothers, and Merrill. Scorsese is evidently much more interested in the criminal aspect of this form of trading, and even here, not so much in the mechanics of IPOs and insider trading, but rather in the spin-off criminality, in the difficulties of money laundering.

Capitalism and form

Now the problem with this analysis of *The Wolf of Wall Street* is that it relies on what the film tells us, on its surface content, in point of fact on a lot of dialogue. Scorsese's films are always chock-a-block with dialogue. So, such an approach is not unfaithful to the film, but a Jamesonian interpretation will always argue that dialectics is to be found in form, in the aesthetics of the film itself. Consider the two bar fight scenes discussed earlier, from *Mean Streets* and *Goodfellas*. I argued that the scenes' implications (in the first film, the scene is followed immediately by a gun battle and then the film ends; in the second film, we only find out later that Tommy is killed for this unauthorized hit) told us something about how the films depicted organized crime. But *Goodfellas* differs from *Mean Streets* in a way that has bearing on our understanding of *The Wolf of Wall Street*. I am talking about the role of plot. In *Goodfellas*, the bar scene picks up on a narrative moment at the beginning of the film. The film's opening (with the title "New York, 1970") shows us Henry, Jimmy, and Tommy driving at night, when they hear a noise from their car. They stop and open the trunk: a man, covered in blood, lies wrapped in sheets. Tommy stabs him with a huge kitchen knife, and Jimmy pulls a handgun, firing off a couple rounds. Henry slams the trunk closed, and, in voice-over, tells us "As far back as I could remember, I always wanted to be a gangster." And with Tony Bennett singing "Rags to Riches," we are suddenly in East New York, Brooklyn, in 1955. So when, an hour later in the film, we return to Billy Batts' murder, the film has solved a narrative enigma (who was in the trunk of the car?), only to open up another one (what will be the effects, who will pay, for this act?).

   If plot is a way of thinking formally about Scorsese's films, how does this work for *The Wolf of Wall Street*? We have, first of all, a jump in the plot at the beginning of the film, which is similar to that in *Goodfellas*. *The Wolf of Wall Street* begins with Belfort already successful, rich, and addicted; then the film moves back to his humble beginnings at Rothschild and the story of how he moves from a Long Island plaza office to that success. Unlike *Goodfellas*, there is not the documentary-like timestamp at the beginning of scenes: the narrative anachrony (as Gerrard Genette refers to such strategies) is more impressionistic.

But there is another pattern to the film that can be analyzed more productively: this has to do with business cycles and the Marxist theory of crisis. Classic Marxism, especially as delineated by Marx in *Capital*, holds that capitalist systems will encounter cyclic crises—in our own time period we can see the Black Monday crisis of 1987, the dot com boom and bust of the late 1990s, and then the subprime mortgage-fuelled crisis of 2008. And is not such a capitalist cycle of crises the very pattern of *The Wolf of Wall Street*'s plot? By this I mean to consider the plot of the film in the broadest of strokes: it moves from Belfort's bucket shop origins to making millions of dollars with an IPO, a pinnacle from which Belfort is then brought down by the twin forces of police attention and his own hubris. But the film closes with Belfort on the rebound, working as a motivational speaker; like the banks of 2008, he was too big to fail.

Here a remark of Bertolt Brecht's is *apropos*:

> Petroleum resists the five-act form; today's catastrophes do not progress in a straight line but in cyclical crises; the "heroes" change with the different phases, are interchangeable, etc.; the graph of people's actions is complicated by abortive actions; fate is no longer a single coherent power; rather there are fields of force which can be seen radiating in opposite directions; the power of groups themselves comprise movements not only against one another but within themselves, etc.[2]

We can take "petroleum" to refer, metonymically, to contemporary capitalism: Brecht's argument is that the form of a given narrative is effected by social conditions (which is no longer a coherent power, it lies in groups and between them). Thus, with Belfort's rise-and-fall-and-rise-and-fall... plot, there any number of determinants, which multiplicity keeps the film from falling into a moralistic narrative, as some critics argue bedevils *Goodfellas*, with Henry Hill's downfall due to his improper appetites.

Consider Belfort's final "fall." The police are investigating his Swiss banker, Jean-Jacques Saurel (Jean Dujardin) for other improprieties, involving the Benihana restaurant chain, and Belfort's underling "Rugrat" is implicated (hence Belfort). So, it is both police interest *and* the Swiss banker's interactions with the Benihana restaurant chain that threaten Belfort, but with the proviso that we see Saurel as himself both inside (part of their criminal conspiracy) and outside (not because of his nationality, but his class position—more on this is discussed below).

The key role of fugazi

But we can also go back to the beginning of the film to understand better the importance to its plot of a fatal misrecognition of the workings of finance capital. In the liquid lunch scene that I keep returning to, Hanna emphasizes the ephemeral nature of their labor: it's *fugazi*, they don't make anything, it's just moving money around. But the film shows that there is a materiality to finance capital: the actual physical money, the $100 bills that they have to do something with. The scene where Brad is taping the money around his girlfriend's body is pornographic alright, but not in the puritanical sense that we see a half-naked woman's body (as already noted, for Jameson, film itself is intrinsically pornographic in how it offers the world up for our gaze). Rather, the woman's body is made "dirty" because now money is taped to it. And that money is in turn made dirty by being returned to the body—both as a gendered body, and as the laboring body.

By returning to the body, the money returns us also to Mark Hanna's body, the body he thumps (and cokes up and masturbates) as a compensation for the lack of body involved in the labor of financial capitalism. More specifically, this narrative arc or plot-form can be seen to constitute a postmodern critique—call it "late Marxism"—of the laborist-substantialist, Second International form of classical Marxism. In that latter formulation, capitalism—American capitalism specifically—was once concerned with making actual things; Fordism, or industrial capitalism, in a kind of melancholic refrain that once upon a time "we made shit," but now, as Hanna tells Belfort, "we don't create shit, we don't build anything." But the problem with this indictment of finance capital is that much the same can be said of postmodern capitalism in general: from the service economy, to the internet, to information cycles. And in this postmodern service economy, labor is both outsourced (a spatial fix, as David Harvey would have it) to the global south, and both there and in the west, often now is ephemeral, immaterial, making not *things* but relations, affects, and the like: from customer service to helpdesks.

This is the meaning of Hanna's speech; but, as the film demonstrates, via its gendering of money (it is as if the brokers' profits, *qua* cash, must be rubbed against women's bodies—there is another scene where Naomi is lying on a bed covered with money), *The Wolf of Wall Street* offers a counter-thesis. But if we are to understand the film, we have to be careful here. Money is not a thing that replaces the "shit" that industrial capitalism once made. It is not so much that the money that the brokers "make"—the "couple mil" as Azoff calls it, which is toted in ubiquitous sports bags, or briefcases but also, in a smuggling scene, in carry-on luggage—it is not so much that this "thingified" money, money which turns out to be an object, is a rebuke to laborist-substantialism in and of itself. Rather, the film offers that money as an analogy for finance capitalism's materiality, an objectness or thingness that is still a matter of exploitation. This is why it is crucial that Belfort fucks on his money, that Brad tapes his money to his girlfriend's body, like a bulletproof vest or, even, a suicide bomber's vest.

Money is an explosive problem in the film, because it carries the taint of sex and drugs. In the film's introduction, after listing his daily intake of pharmaceuticals, Belfort continues, "But of all the drugs under god's blue heaven, there is one that is my absolute favorite," and he chops up some cocaine with a razor blade. "See," he tells us, "enough of this shit will make you invincible, able to conquer the world, and eviscerate your enemies." Belfort then snorts the coke through a rolled-up hundred dollar bill, and clarifies, "I'm not talking about this"—gesturing at the cocaine—"I'm talking about this"—snapping the bill, before crumpling it up and tossing it into a wastebasket. And again, this is not a moral critique: brokers are not less human because they pay for sex or use drugs. Those intoxicants are themselves marks of that exploitation that underlies capitalism: in the logic of the film, in the logic of its plot-form, money, an embodiment of profit, is smeared with coke and sexual fluids (and so must be disposed of: thrown in the garbage, flown out of the country).

So, here we have an interpretive problem that is also a political one: why is money so hard to move around, why is it such a recalcitrant part of the film's plot? Is it, as I am arguing here, because it stands in for the "shit" that we no longer make (the ubiquitous nature of the signifier "shit" itself adds an excremental dimension to these questions)? Or is the money "tainted" by its association with drugs and sex, rendering the film's critique a moral one? Or, finally—and this is the argument I am trying to make here—is the role of the money in the film's plot both (and neither) of these things at the same time? The money is an object in the plot because the film's subject, finance capitalism, no longer makes "shit," but finance capital nonetheless still "makes" exploitation, the traces of which exploitation, via bodies, resurfaces in sex and drugs, and thus (the money) will function in that plot as both spur and impediment, both cause and effect.

Again, it is important to realize how this thesis functions cinematically. Take the film's use of "fugazi": Hanna, before he tells Belfort that "we don't create shit, we don't build anything," says, "It's all a *fugazi*, you know what a *fugazi* is?" Here Hanna pronounces it with a short *a*. To which Belfort answers "No, *fugazi*, it's a fake." Belfort pronounces it with a long *a*. And Hanna comes back pronouncing the word both ways: "*Fugazi, fugazi*, it's a wahzi it's a woozy, it's fairy dust, it doesn't exist, it's never landed, it's no matter, it's not on the elemental chart, it's not fucking real." Now, Hanna's pronunciation is that of the Washington, D.C. hardcore band Fugazi (which apparently comes from a Vietnam War slang term for "Fucked-up, got ambushed, zipped into a body bag"). And Belfort's is the pronunciation used in *Donnie Brasco* (Newell, 1997), when Donnie (Johnny Depp) tells Lefty (Al Pacino) that the diamond ring he's trying to sell is fugazy, a fake (an NYC mob slang term, derived from commercials for the Fugazy limousine service in the 1970s). In spelling and pronunciation, the fakery inherent in the stock market, turns out to be deeply dialectical.

Class on Wall Street

As we saw in the previous chapter, Jameson argues for the continued relevance of class in discussing contemporary culture: class understood not as an identity but as a representation. Or better: class as a relationship. Thus, the first way to think about class in *The Wolf of Wall Street* is to contrast it with identity politics, which, in Scorsese criticism, inevitably means to talk about masculinity (and ethnic masculinity in particular). If the archetypal Scorsesean anti-hero is a white ethnic working-class male uneasy in his masculinity, then Jordan Belfort can more accurately be said to embody that subjectivity with respect to class. But if we turn to questions of relationality, these categories can be fine-tuned in terms of the residual ideologeme of the gangster in the picture—the gangster, and his brocialist other, in terms of *réssentiment*.

That relationality is also what is at work in how the film figures Stratton Oakmont with respect to so-called "white shoe" firms, the prestigious Wall Street companies that would soon, between the time period of the film proper and its release, come to stand in the popular imagination both as the perpetrators of the 2008 crisis and, via the logic of "too big to fail," its beneficiaries. Finally, class is figured with Belfort's fitful role, in the final act of the film, as informer, a privileged trope of recent cinema. Class is not simply a matter of relation or status, Jameson tells us, it is also about struggle, and nowhere is that struggle more apparent than in Belfort's attempts *not* to be a class traitor, not to be a snitch.

A standard trope of Scorsese criticism is to focus on his male heroes (or anti-heroes) as embodying a crisis of late-twentieth-century masculinity. Think of Travis Bickle wandering the streets of New York (*Taxi Driver*, 1975), Jake LaMotta's bruised and battered body (*Raging Bull*, 1980), Henry Hill's always-on-the-outside Italian-Irish gangster in *Goodfellas*, even Newland Archer (*The Age of Innocence*, 1993), enjoying not getting the object of his desire. These characters all depict in no uncertain terms a male subjectivity very far from the standard Hollywood hero of the period—whether the action flick's Stallone or Schwarzenegger or the sensitive film's Woody Allen or Alan Alda. Or perhaps it is more accurate to say that Scorsese's men are the dialectical outcome of a cinema that veers from action hero to sensitive male: Scorsese's men *act* out because they can't *figure* it out. This is an impressive strain of Scorsese criticism (for more of which see *Further Reading* at the end of this book), but its tenor ignores, for the most part, Jameson's warnings about mistaking class for a thing that then is represented in a film (in the sense of positive or negative representations). Rather, Jameson argues, class is a problem, a problem that is not so much addressed by actual representation but by new interpretive methodologies.

Class as a concept, as enunciated in key texts such as *The Communist Manifesto*, is not so much a matter of a local identity or its ethnography—the question of authentic Italian-American representation in Scorsese's films, for instance. Scorsese has himself said he likes to cast Italian-American

actors for certain roles for the authentic lifeways they bring
to their roles—but this realism as always, in his films, conflicts
with their more expressionist tendencies. These postmodern
elements of Scorsese include the use of soundtrack "needle-
drops," the super-8 home movies that begin *Mean Streets*, that
movie's and countless other's quotation of older Hollywood,
the TV *and* fantasy sequences in *The King of Comedy*, the
fantasy Christ has on the cross in *The Last Temptation*, his
outright fantastic films (*Kundun* [1997], *Shutter Island* [2010],
Hugo [2011]), set shots with appearing/disappearing props
(*The Age of Innocence*, *The Wolf of Wall Street*), and general
post-genre hipness with monster-*noir* stills, cowboy sepia
Sergio Leone, and Hitchcock archness.

I will come back to these postmodern tendencies in *The
Wolf of Wall Street* later, but for now I want to mark a break
with the uneasy male hero of early Scorsese. Jordan Belfort
wears his class position confidently with a mix of paranoia.
He is remarkably akin to Rupert Pupkin in *The King of
Comedy*; in both cases the paranoia is no less a matter of
réssentiment than also an accurate "metric." Belfort is
pursued as much by his own addictions, his own cravings,
as he is by the authorities. But as with Pupkin, the paranoia
is both accurate and inaccurate: for Belfort makes millions
before and after his prison time (incarceration is a form of
commons, the brief moment when the people get their due; it
is a form of restitution). Belfort's iteration of male confidence
(which is also a cluelessness) both is and is not historical.
Or, perhaps, Rupert Pupkin's confidence was linked to the
psychotic masculine of the Travis Bickle/John Hinckley, Jr.—
the declassed, postindustrial male, alone in the city, striking
out violently (*The King of Comedy* was being made during the
trial of Hinckley, who claimed inspiration from *Taxi Driver*
for his 1981 attempted assassination of President Reagan).
But, crucially, Belfort is not alone: perhaps, the fact that
Jordan Belfort essentially has to assemble a crew to help him
"take" Wall Street shows the necessity of collective working-
class action (which used to be called revolution).

Let's go to work

Working-class collectivity is deployed at two key moments in *The Wolf of Wall Street:* a restaurant table scene where we meet Belfort's crew that he puts together to run his own shop, and a short scene immediately afterwards when the same men stand as if posing for mug shots in their postindustrial workplace. Restaurant scenes are a common trope for American films to establish male characters' bona fides: from *Diner* (Barry Levinson, 1982) to *Do the Right Thing* (Spike Lee, 1989) to *Reservoir Dogs* (Tarantino, 1992), men sitting around a diner or greasy spoon breakfast table as a public collectivity, a demonstration of their power (however circumscribed). The diner table is a public space that is also private, a space often featuring traditional gender roles, such as female servers. Think of *Alice Doesn't Live Here Anymore* (1974), Scorsese's first "women's film," or the scene in *Reservoir Dogs* where Mr. Pink (Steve Buscemi) rails against an inattentive waitress and Mr. White (Harvey Keitel) defends the said occupation.

The restaurant scene comes after Belfort has met Donnie Azoff, they have found a former auto body shop to take over for their office, and he now has to assemble his sales team. Belfort turns, he tells us, to his "hometown boys," and the restaurant scene begins, scored by Billy Joel's "Movin' Out." So, we are very much in a suburban milieu here (Joel is the veritable bard of Long Island), as we meet Sea Otter (Henry Zebrowski), "who sold meat, and weed," Chester (Kenneth Choi), "who sold tires, and weed," and Robbie (Brian Sacca), "who sold anything he could get his hands on, mostly weed."

Singled out here—for reasons that are crucial to questions of class in the film—is Brad (Jon Bernthal), who is such a successful drug dealer already ("the Quaalude king of Bayside") that "he didn't go along with us." Introductions are accomplished with a roving camera eye that only cuts away to a vignette in Brad's backyard as he pumps iron and sells Ludes to teenagers (the Billy Joel track continues uninterrupted, establishing the backyard scene's secondary relationship to the restaurant).

Belfort now warms up his crew, telling them that people want to get rich for nothing—referring to, after he is interrupted by Sea Otter's example of an Amish exception, "normal people, working class everyday people." The crew interrupts each other with digressions about nuns and Buddhists—it is telling that religion functions both as a release for humor and as a way to not talk about business—and then Belfort offers an object lesson, telling Brad to sell him a pen. Brad takes the pen, asks Belfort to write down his name, and so Belfort needs his pen back. The lesson is "supply and demand," or, as Belfort tells his crew, they need to create a sense of urgency with their customers. Belfort will return to this object lesson at the film's conclusion, when he is leading a seminar in New Zealand, and asks audience members to sell him a pen.

As much of a cinematic trope the diner scene is, it is filmed naturalistically, which means, following Scorsese's dialectics of realism and expressionism, we soon see the characters introduced again in a more meta-cinematic way. As Belfort looks out over his men working in the barely converted auto body shop, he admits that they are not Harvard MBAs, and we then see the men stand, one at a time, in front of a cinderblock wall as Belfort insults them. This shorter sequence carries the connotation of a combination of audition shots and police video surveillance. And unlike the restaurant scene, here we are in a private space, a private space that is also a workplace. While a restaurant is a workplace for serving staff and cooks, the Stratton Oakmont space is the workplace for the crew: soon they are working the phones.

My argument thus far with respect to class in *The Wolf of Wall Street* is that the film is a departure from the classic Scorsese working-class antihero, in that here Belfort is part of a collective, has assembled a crew. (I will return to this topic, the assembling of a crew, when I discuss the film's Utopian dimensions below). Now, by calling his sales team a "crew" I am suggesting that they are akin to a criminal collectivity. I would argue that *The Wolf of Wall Street* is very much a gangster picture, especially in the vein of *Goodfellas* and

Casino, where the protagonists are undone as much by their own narco-appetites as by such external forces as the police (in *Goodfellas*) or mob rivals (in *Casino*). Perhaps this is too certain a declaration; but I want to explore it with respect to class in two different ways: first, through flipping Jameson's declaration that *The Godfather* can be interpreted as a movie about American business practices; second, by arguing that Brad's character's function illustrates precisely this ambiguity.

As we saw in Chapter 1, Jameson argues that while gangsters in the 1930s and 1940s were either "sick" psychopaths of Jimmy Cagney variety or *film noir* loners who bore the burden of wartime trauma, with *The Godfather*, the mob was now a corporate entity, and so stood in for the depersonalized violence of multinational capitalism. But *The Godfather* shows us the elite of the mob world, Don Corleone and his family, whereas Scorsese's gangster pictures first of all looked at the "soldiers," Charlie in *Mean Streets* and Henry in *Goodfellas*: these are a working-class Mafia. Even *Casino*, which shows Midwestern bookie Ace Rothstein (Robert de Niro) take control of a Vegas hotel in the 1970s, is still very much about a middle manager—not the corporate elite.

This classed nature of Scorsese's pictures then allows us to better understand the importance to how *The Wolf of Wall Street* reverses Jameson's thesis: the film argues that finance capital itself is a form of high-level gangsterism. This argument is not simply an observation of the actual laws broken by Stratton Oakmont—pump and dumps, insider trading, money laundering—nor the ethics of "literally selling garbage to garbage men." Rather, finance capitalism is gangsterism in the sense that it is a violent system that encourages impossible economic dreams instead of actual social change, a system that sets up the accumulation of profit from the buying and selling of stocks, little more than legalized gambling at the highest level.

Key to this understanding of *The Wolf of Wall Street* is the character Brad. As we already saw in the restaurant scene, Brad is both inside Belfort's crew and outside it. He is making enough money selling Quaaludes that he does not need to become a broker. But he continues to help Belfort, delivering a sports bag (of drugs? money?) to a golf party, holding proxy stocks, offering his girlfriend's body—and later her family—to help smuggle money to Switzerland. Brad is the most ethnically marked character in the film: often standing around barechested, he usually wears a large Jewish *Chai* necklace—unlike the other "out" Jew in the picture, Donnie Azoff (Jonah Hill), who wears horn rim glasses with clear lenses to look more WASP. This ethnic antagonism is performed during the golf course scene when Brad, spotting Azoff in his pink argyle sweater vest, asks him, "Who you supposed to be, Jack Nickel Jew?" Ethnicity is related in these characters' antagonisms to the question of legitimate business. To use Jameson's language from his essay on *Dog Day Afternoon*, ethnicity is an *analogon* for gangsterism: the more ethnic one is, the more of a gangster.

The more ethnic you are, the more gangster

So, Brad's role is complex, just as the film's thesis with respect to gangsterism and finance capital is complex. The more money that Belfort and his crew make, the more of a problem it is: hence the turn to money laundering, shipping the money overseas to the proverbial Swiss bank. Again, this plot element offers a reversal of the usual Mafia logic, where a legitimate business will be a "front" for the mob; here, Brad is the Mafia that is required by a legitimate undertaking. But this necessity for a criminal element, for the gangster to be part of business, is also a problem, as shown in the ongoing battle between Brad and Azoff.

The conflict begins when Brad is taping bundles of cash to his girlfriend's halfnaked body in a harebrained scheme to smuggle the money. Realizing the futility of that plan, he suggests they enlist her entire family, all of whom have Swiss passports. Azoff, insouciant, reminds Brad not to forget about his money ("I got a couple mil coming in like a week"), that he will give him a call and Brad can come pick it up. Brad takes Belfort outside to vent, telling him that he's no *Schwarze*, he *doesn't* do pick ups, that *he* will choose the meeting place and that Azoff had better come "correct," and that if he comes "loopy," Brad will mash his teeth in. Azoff overhears this, and starts insulting Brad in turn, even after Brad has pulled a gun. Azoff tells Brad that he is just a "pill dealer" and that he has "five more just like" him, at which point Brad punches him out, finishing the scene with homophobic slurs.

And when Azoff, a scene later, arrives at a meeting with Brad, he is in bad shape, swerving into a shopping center parking lot in his Rolls-Royce, barely able to exit the car. This, it turns out, is an act, but Brad is still unimpressed, and the seasoned gangster tells Azoff that his driving will attract police attention. As Azoff now engages in homophobic taunts of Brad, their escalating brouhaha does indeed attract the attention of a passing police cruiser. Azoff escapes, and Brad goes to jail.

There are two aspects of this confrontation that will help us to understand how it contributes to a reading of the class dimensions of *The Wolf of Wall Street*. First, it confirms our thesis that Brad embodies a gangster, but also working class, subjectivity, a subjectivity that must be contained or expelled from the crew. Later in the film, we see Brad in a brief scene after his release from prison: as he is fêted on Belfort's yacht, in the voice-over Belfort tells us that Brad no longer wanted to be part of his crew, and that two years later he was dead. Brad cannot be part of the crew—he knows this—as an example of what Jameson calls the *non-dit* or the "political unconscious" of the film, which I will further explore later in this chapter.

The exchange also helps us to map out how the film figures class in terms of both its generic signals (finance film? gangster film?) and who must be eliminated or removed from the scene (in this case, Brad). The film posits the necessary conjunction of capital (or finance) and violence: a position occupied by Wolf, by Belfort (even if he does not seem to be directly violent himself, he exhorts his brokers to be "telephone terrorists," to use their phones like AK-47s). Then, gangsters, who stand in for workers, are themselves doomed *only* to be violent (again, this is an ideal position: remember that Brad does not join

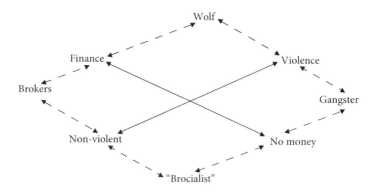

FIGURE 2.1 *Character analysis of* The Wolf of Wall Street.

Belfort's crew because he is already making lots of money selling Quaaludes). Brokers have some access to money, but they are in the end nonviolent (or their violence is the symbolic kind of breaking baseball bats on the brokerage floor). The lowest position is that of the Marxist, the "brocialist," who, trapped in an identity politics present, is neither violent nor rich.

What is also relevant is the role of homophobia in Brad's exchanges with Azoff. When Azoff tells Brad that he can pick up his (that is, Azoff's) money, he is sitting in an almost camp gesture, limp wrist and all. Then, when Brad punches Azoff in the mouth, he calls him a "faggot." And in the parking lot scene, Azoff mock-accuses Brad of homosexual tendencies ("did you try to kiss me, bro?"), following it up with the standard disavowal: "I said a homophobic thing, you're just not the one for me." The violence of the language here indicates the stakes at work. First of all, there is a certain realism at work (heterosexual men are still given to such outbursts), but also a responsibility that the film must take for its own portrayal. And yet these utterances are also an indication of the difficulties the film has in its figuring of working-class collectivities: given the homosocial nature of the brokerage (only one female broker has any kind of speaking role in the film), it is ideologically easy to confuse class struggle with other forms of camaraderie.

Wall Street's band of outsiders

I remarked above that ethnicity functions as an analogon for gangsterism (and, thereby, class) in the Brad/Azoff antagonism; Jameson's concept finds a stronger form in the question of the (class) relationship between Stratton Oakmont and Wall Street proper. The class dimension of how finance capital functions in the film runs, then, from the proper, prestigious, "white shoe" firm of L.F. Rothschild, where Belfort has a short career; then from the Long Island "bucket shop" located in a strip plaza, where he begins his career again, "selling garbage to garbage men"; and finally the transformation of that firm into Stratton Oakmont, the better to sell garbage to the 1 percent. Thinking of how class functions in the finance business sector can rapidly become identitarian, however, fixated on ethnographies of bluebloods versus parvenus, sort of Paul Fussell meets Pierre Bourdieu, with some Tom Wolfe thrown in for "thick" description. And if social class predicts the criminality of Belfort et al., how to account for ruling class criminality, unless with a revolutionary moralism?

Here, two ruling class characters suggest divergent (or even dialectical) ways in which the rulers approach gangsterism. The Swiss banker we have already met, Jean-Jacques Saurel, is suavely accommodating and also follows his own carnal habits: this is the latest version of the dissipated aristocrat. But Naomi's aunt Emma (Joanna Lumley, of *AbFab* fame) is a world-weary maternal figure, almost Brechtian in her resistance to Belfort's French-kissing lasciviousness (but not the general larceny: aunt Emma does the criminal work with grim purpose, not with enjoyment). If aunt Emma functions as a maternal figure in the film, the father is played by Rob Reiner, who brings to the picture his own actorly repressed (he acts very much like the father that was Archie Bunker from the 1970s series *All in the Family* [Norman Lear, 1971–1979], Reiner acted in) as well as a *soupçon* of 1980s NYC crime TV. This last scene appears in clips from *The Equalizer* (Michael

Sloan, Richard Lindheim, 1985–1989), which Belfort Sr. watches even as his telephone rings.

But I am still considering here the argument that class is figured in this film via the analogon of Wall Street firms: the antagonism between prestigious "white shoe" firms, and Belfort's Long Island upstart. This is certainly the thesis put forward by Belfort in the first of two key yacht scenes: when the FBI agent Patrick Denham (Kyle Chandler) visits him on his yacht (the second key scene is the storm in the Mediterranean). When Denham arrives at the boat, Belfort welcomes him aboard with all sorts of temptations, from food and alcohol to his bikini-clad Stratton girls. But Denham wants to get down to business, and so does Belfort, passing over a list of the guests at his wedding (the FBI has subpoenaed the wedding video as evidence). Denham and Belfort do a little verbal sparring, with Belfort professing that he doesn't know why his company is being investigated, but admitting that Stratton Oakmont is "a little unorthodox" and that it is "a little loud in the way we do things." They are "the new guys on the block … trying to make a name for ourselves," and that they are, in a mixed metaphor, "banging on Wall Street's door." Denham seems to concur, saying that the case was dropped on his desk, and that he needs to make a show of looking at Stratton as a new company that is getting press.

At this point, Belfort makes a very interesting claim, telling Denham that "you should see what's going on at the bigger firms … Goldman, Lehman Brothers, Merrill, collateralized debt obligations." Now, no doubt Belfort's protests here must be read with a grain of salt—or at least dialectically. On the one hand, they are true to the vibe of the film, which time and again stresses Stratton's outsider bona fides (the Long Island crew, the auto body shop). And yet we are, in this scene, on a yacht with Belfort surrounded by luxury, and this talk of being a "new company" and "knocking on doors" can sound like rationalization. But, again, Belfort's attitude, of the newcomer or outsider, is of a piece with Scorsese's filmic history: Charlie trying to climb the Mafia ladder in *Mean Streets*, Rupert

Pupkin waiting at the stage door in *The King of Comedy*, Henry doomed, by his Irish/Italian heritage, to never being a "made man" in *Goodfellas*.

Be that as it may, there is a narrative or ideological titbit in the yacht scene, when Belfort offers some inside dirt on the prestigious companies, and their "collateralized debt obligations." Also called CDOs, these obscure financial instruments were a key element in the subprime mortgage debacle, which in turn precipitated the financial crisis of 2008. As explained by former regulator Sheila Bair (of the FDIC), CDOs were a "tranche" or slice of the highest risk (but also a higher return) of a bundle of mortgages. These CDOs themselves were often further sliced and speculated upon as "synthetic" CDOs; finally, many investors who purchased CDOs would also buy insurance against losses there via Credit Default Swaps, or CDS. When predatory lending practices in the early 2000s, coupled with a housing bubble that finally burst, led to many mortgage holders defaulting (the subprime crisis of 2007), CDOs and CDS were key instruments in that process, even driving the process. The market for CDOs meant that mortgage brokers were highly incentivized, and so between 2003 and 2007 housing prices in the United States rose by 27 percent, with $4 trillion in mortgage securities and $700 billion in CDOs. And as if to confirm Belfort's claim, "Merrill Lynch, Goldman Sachs, and the securities arm of Citigroup accounted for more than 30 percent of CDOs structured from 2004 to 2007."[3]

Informers as class traitors

This financial security arcana thus serves two purposes: first, it provides a historical context for what is otherwise purely imaginary *réssentiment* on the part of Belfort. Stratton Oakmont's crimes pale against those of the subprime mortgage crisis. But it also places Belfort in company with other informants both in the Scorsese canon (Henry Hill, but also undercover agent and police "mole" in *The Departed*) and contemporary film in general: *Donnie Brasco*, Mr. Orange in *Reservoir Dogs*, and *Internal Affairs* (Andy Lau, Alan Mak, 2002), the Hong Kong *policier* on which *The Departed* was based.

The snitch or informant is a cultural trope in recent film no doubt for many reasons: psychoanalytic notions of the "split subject," contemporary feelings that we are being pulled asunder by the demands of everyday life, but also, I think, because in many ways the informant's dilemma helps us to think about class and, specifically, loyalties. The informant is a figure for the class traitor—for someone who has "betrayed" his or her class of origin. To better understand this dynamic, consider the two kinds of informants or snitches: the undercover police officer (as in *Donnie Brasco*, *Reservoir Dogs*, *The Departed*, and *Internal Affairs*) and the criminal who turns "state's evidence" (as in *Goodfellas* and *The Wolf of Wall Street*). The undercover officer often will be figured as suffering from ethical dilemmas even as he or she betrays their comrades, their fellow criminals. This is the conundrum that *Donnie Brasco* portrays, and *Reservoir Dogs*, when Harvey Keitel's character, realizing he has been protecting a "rat" (Tim Roth), shoots him in the head.

This ethical dilemma does not play out in the same way in *The Wolf of Wall Street*, and I will argue that this is because of two reasons: first, class solidarity, and second, Belfort's psychopathology. The film's final forty-five minutes is an extended sequence of subpoenas, interrogation, and attempted wiretapping. First of all, Belfort and Stratton brokers are brought into the SEC for questioning: they all deny any knowledge of the Steve Madden deal, of telephone calls to clients, and so on (one character's claim, "I have no recommendation of that," both plays off his stupidity and the similarity of a stock *recommendation* and his denial of a *recollection*). Then, after further mayhem, Belfort agrees to wear a wire and to name his coconspirators.

Again, he tries to game the system (over sushi, he passes a note to Donnie Azoff, telling him he is wearing a wire and not to incriminate himself), but in the end Belfort does name everyone, leading to the indictment of two dozen, and receives a three-year sentence. Our film then, rather than depicting a rat's divided loyalties (an interiorization of the class betrayal), shows Belfort trying to evade precisely this betrayal, but caught in the consequences of his own lifestyle (even after going sober, he has stashed cocaine in a sofa cushion, for example). The morality of the film is then more political than, say *Goodfellas*, or other gangster films in which a criminal is punished because of their excess.

To illustrate this final argument with respect to class in *The Wolf of Wall Street* I consider the scene where Belfort, about to step down from Stratton Oakmont, announces in a speech to his brokers that he will stay on. After first saying he is leaving the company in the hands of Donnie Azoff, Belfort tells a story of how he loaned a female broker (Stephanie Kurtzuba) money when she first started. This tale of his own generosity triggers a change of heart for Belfort, and so he rescinds his resignation, and the crowd goes wild.

This is also to argue with or against Jameson's contention that we err if we look to collective figurations in film (Sonny exhorting the crowds to chant "Attica," in reference to recent riots at the New York state prison, in *Dog Day Afternoon*) as a form of class representation. Or at least to fine-tune his argument, what is "collective" about such representations in *The Wolf of Wall Street* is not so much that they are showing contemporary, postmodern labor (working the phone, in an open plan office, ubiquitous mid-1990s off-white computer monitors) but that such collective labor is itself mediatized. There are quite a few scenes in the film where Belfort addresses his brokers, beginning with his *Moby-Dick* speech, culminating in the Steve Madden IPO, and then this final address, where, perhaps, notions of solidarity help to gird his loins in a battle against class betrayal. But these scenes, and the question of their mediatization, are better explored under the larger questions of postmodernism in *The Wolf of Wall Street*, to which I now turn.

Is *The Wolf of Wall Street* a postmodern film?

To talk about *The Wolf of Wall Street* in terms of post-modernism is first of all to deal with modernism and with the question of these aesthetic periodizations that characterize Jameson's thought but also contemporary cultural theory. And if postmodernism as an approach means to consider form in terms of history, then we perhaps can most productively think about *The Wolf of Wall Street* in terms of pastiche, or its habit of appropriating (with the aim of "volatilization") other media forms like the TV commercial. But lest postmodernism be simply a checklist, we can also attend to the film's spectacularizing of labor—with Belfort's mediatized speeches to his employees—and to the role, in this "late" Scorsese film, of such tricks as self-reflexive camera work and the voice-over, its status as an adaptation of Belfort's memoir, and some trademark features of the Jamesonian postmodern.

Scorsese: Modern or postmodern?

So, to begin with the question of whether *The Wolf of Wall Street* is a postmodern film is to attempt to situate Scorsese's film—but also his *oeuvre*—in the historical and aesthetic paradigms raised by Jameson in his writings. More specifically, we can think of whether the film meets the criteria laid out by Jameson in his postmodernism essay: in terms of its opposition to modernism, notions of pastiche and the death of the subject, a break down of boundaries between high and low culture, and an attempt to think historically after what would soon be called "the end of history." Scorsese's films straddle the modern–postmodern divide. Such early movies as *Mean Streets* and *Taxi Driver* are still late modernist films, reworking classic Hollywood cinema. A clip from *The Searchers* (1956) appears on a TV screen in *Mean Streets*, and that

John Ford Western arguably is the *Ur*-text for *Taxi Driver*. Like John Wayne, de Niro's Travis Bickle is trying to save a woman (Jodi Foster) from savage treachery. The parallel between New York's squalid Hell's Kitchen and the American West is even more pat if we think of geographer Neil Smith's writings on gentrification, which trenchantly take apart the rhetoric of the "pioneer" in urban renewal. But Scorsese's films, even as they introduce rock and doo-wop alongside Neapolitan love songs, nonetheless remain modernist in their *Nouvelle Vague* camera work, ambiguous anti-heros, and moderate self-reflexivity. They are still, in critic Robin Wood's term, a "coherent text" (that Wood, writing in the 1970s, could only see *Taxi Driver* as an "incoherent text" is due to his residual *auteurism:* for him, the film is the result of a conflict between Scorsese and his screenwriter, Paul Schrader).

As much as Scorsese's gangster films are a thematic precursor to *The Wolf of Wall Street*, it is arguably *The King of Comedy* that provides the strongest formal analogue, from its televisual framing to the role of Rupert Pupkin's fantasies. Here, but also in *Goodfellas*, modernist filmmaking has been jettisoned in favor of narrative free-for-all and cipher-like characters. Why do Pupkin—or Henry Hill—do what they do? Because they are in a Scorsese film. The strongest argument to be made in terms of a modernist–postmodern genealogy of Scorsese's film, or of *The Wolf of Wall Street* in that canon, lies in a comparison with how the film differs in its practice of quotation from *Mean Streets*. Where the latter film will quote lovingly from *The Searchers*, *The Big Heat* (Fritz Lang, 1953), and *Tomb of Ligeia* (Roger Corman, 1965), *The Wolf of Wall Street* merely cites television commercials. *The Wolf of Wall Street* has abandoned cinema: the volatilization of its ontology means that it is barely a film in the new media landscape. This is an argument I develop further below; at this point, I merely want to indicate that key difference with respect to quotation and pastiche.

The difference is this: in *Mean Streets* (which, for the purposes of this argument, I posit as a late modernist film), films are quoted in a contained way. When Charlie and his buddies come into some money, "let's go to the movies," he says, and the next shot is a clip, a fight in *The Searchers*. Charlie and his friends are watching the film in a movie theater, and the scene is played for laughs as we hear an altercation between other patrons. After the climactic bar scene, Charlie and Johnny go to a movie, and we see a clip from *Tomb of Ligeia*, and our characters are now tense (Johnny biting his nails) as they watch the horror film. At the film's climax, after Charlie and Johnny Boy have been shot by a loan shark's thug (played by Scorsese), we see Charlie's uncle, watching an apposite scene from *The Big Heat*. In these three scenes where *Mean Streets* quotes from another film, the quotation itself is given narrative coherence; in the first two instances, the characters say "let's go to the movies" or are told to "go to a movie." If filmgoing is a social activity that offers release from the everyday (but also from danger)—and it is also a form of mimetic desire, as with the gangster uncle watching a gangster film—it does not upset the framing narrative, the film that is *Mean Streets*.

Consider, in contrast, the Jordan Belfort "Straight Line" commercial in *The Wolf of Wall Street*. Posing in front of a mansion, and then on a yacht, Belfort tells the viewer that it is possible to be "financially independent," and that "all you need is a strategy." Ordinary-looking folks testify to the success of Belfort's sales seminars, and we see Belfort emerge from a helicopter, only to be arrested by the FBI ("I'm fucking shooting a fucking infomercial here you fucking cock-suckers" he exclaims). When an agent approaches the camera and puts his hand over the lens, the camera tilts to the ground, and, the picture at a 90 degree angle, Belfort is marched out of view. Then, with Plastic Bertrand's "Ca plane pour moi" playing, Belfort is given his mug shot, and he tells us via voice-over that he was arrested because of an unrelated money laundering involving "Rocky Aoki," founder of the Benihana restaurant chain—for which we then see a commercial, as Belfort rails against this apparent injustice. "Why God," Belfort asks, "would you be so cruel as to choose a chain of hibachi restaurants to take me down?"

Now this sequence of scenes that runs from Belfort's mock infomercial to the actual Benihana commercial is no masterpiece of cinema: it is hurried exposition, showing arrests, mug shots, and sets that are only on screen for a second or two. But the media logic is impeccable. First we have a commercial playing—a specific kind of commercial, the 1980s or 1990s genre of the infomercial, which, playing late at night in those decades, would sell everything from hair-cutting vacuum attachments to real estate scams. So, not only a television genre, not only a television genre of marketing, but even lower, arguably the lowest form of media at the time. And yet designed to sell hope, to sell luxury or the idea of luxury. But as the helicopter touches down (a bit wobbly: we wonder if a coked-up Belfort is at the helm), "reality" in the form of the FBI intrudes. Is this a case, as Jameson argues, of film demonstrating its superiority over TV? Does the film blurring the boundaries between its own narrative and a fictionalized TV commercial show the prowess of cinema? Or remind us, as we were getting sucked into the infomercial (yeah, I'd like to make more money!), of the surrounding narrative? If so, then what do we do with the *actual* commercial that comes a minute or two later, a commercial for a company whose founder helps to bring down Belfort? And, does it matter whether Aoki and Benihana actually were part of Belfort's downfall? These very questions of interpretation show us that the effect of the commercials, whether as pastiche or actual quotation, is to dissolve the film's very ontology. And this is what makes the film deeply postmodern.

Commercials against themselves

But we are not finished with considering how commercials function in the film. Take, for instance, the film's opening. As noted in the synopsis on the first pages of this book, *The Wolf of Wall Street* begins with a commercial for Stratton Oakmont, a tranquil commercial that within thirty seconds cuts away to a debauched scene in the same firm: dwarf-tossing and the like. *This is what Wall Street* is really about, the cut tells us: not those respectable, honest, suit-clad brokers helping you make money. Rather, they get together in obscene cabals, offer insufferable indignities to the disabled freaks, and, as shown elsewhere in the film, engage in the drug and prostitution alluded to above, with the added lascivious bonus of a great deal of female nudity (and the odd exposed penis).

Such a thesis is no doubt part of what *The Wolf of Wall Street* is concerned with, a libidinized version of Occupy Wall Street or Thomas Piketty's *Capital*, even if we have already argued that such a critique is in danger of lapsing into moralizing. But consider what is happening formally with *The Wolf of Wall Street*'s opening. The film offers two different forms of representation of the financial industry: the industry's own via the television commercial, and art, or cinema's representation, through the carnal office party. And then remember the argument that Jameson makes about *The Parallax View*, with respect to film's "rivalry with another medium," that there is a sort of sibling rivalry at work, which end up affirming film's "ontological primacy." As *The Wolf of Wall Street* shows us, this setting off of trans-medial antagonisms has three implications: first, the conflict of media over representational efficacy or veracity (this will be how *The Wolf of Wall Street* defines "ontological primacy"); second, a post-cinema situating of its narrative in the commercial landscape of mutable delivery modes: in the multiplex, on DVD, streamed or downloaded; third, a critique of representation itself (or at least an argument with respect to the medium specificity of representation that aligns it with the other strategies mentioned above: Belfort's speeches, Scorsese's self-reflexivity).

These three interpretive arguments are themselves worth examining. Consider Jameson's "ontological primacy." At first this thesis seems unobjectionable: *yes*, film is superior to advertising, *of course* a Scorsese film will show what Wall Street is "really like" in comparison to a genre that exists merely to attract clients. But that thesis is problematic precisely for how closely it hews to the content or message of the film (the carnality of Wall Street), and so we should be attentive to moments which challenge the formal argument. Here I can think of two right off the bat: the use of documentary imagery in the commercial, and the role of the lion. First, the film's opening commercial turns out to incorporate footage shot on Wall Street and in the financial district, introducing, if not the Real, some semblance of the same, into its otherwise mendacious message. Then, what is the lion doing in the shot, walking between desks? In the commercial's voice-over, we are told that the investment world is a jungle, and thus we see images of the bull and bear sculptures on Wall Street that embody the "bull market," when stock values are rising, and the "bear market," when they are falling. Presumably Stratton Oakmont has tamed the wild beasts of finance capitalism for the benefit of its clients. Perhaps that same lion is what returns as the carnality of the dwarf-tossing scene: perhaps there is a more complicated relationship between commercials and film than previously argued.

These qualifications help us to sharpen the thesis: Jameson's argument from *The Geopolitical Aesthetic* that the juxtaposition of media asserts a primacy is Hegelian. He is talking about dialectics here. This argument comes out of his longstanding critique of postmodernism. Unlike the standard argument that the collage, sampling, and mash-ups of contemporary culture are a liberating cross-over of media, forms, and high and low, Jameson detects an antagonism at work, an antagonism that is both formal (having to do with the aesthetics of the film in question) and political (a matter not only of class struggle but, finally, the question of modes of production). The opening commercial is not the only one in the film: we also see snippets from real commercials, for Steve Madden shoes, and the Benihana Japanese steak house. These commercials, again, serve a documentary purpose: they remind viewers that the film is based on real events, on a "true story." So, now we have two different kinds of commercials, of media, being entertained in the film: the real and the simulated. Scorsese's film means we must revise Jameson's thesis with respect to media ontology, and rather than seeing the appearance of TV advertisements as an assertion of postmodern, borderless aesthetics, we can instead posit that the juxtaposition stages their incommensurability, their antagonism.

But what of the second meaning I offer of the juxtaposed media: the nesting or framing of narrative levels accomplished by the film in its beginning with a commercial? Today films arrive not only shot through with product placements and other detritus of commercial culture (as film adapts not only novels and comic books but also toys and video games and theme park rides), but are also, importantly, framed in almost every form of distribution by commercials, be they the ads, cinema audience games, and trailers that preface cinematic releases, more of the same on the DVD, or those surrounding the screen/browser as one watches or downloads on a digital device. These commercial frames further erode the distinction between a film proper and its fiduciary surroundings; to put it more simply, we are never quite sure where a film begins or ends, either temporally (and now we often wait until after the credits to see a blooper or out-take reel), or spatially (we watch a film even while ads for other films surround it in the web browser). If this is the media ecology into which *The Wolf of Wall Street* emerges, by beginning with a commercial, it criticizes such an ecology even as it enacts it. Is the opening commercial part of the film or just one more ad? It is both, and that is the point.

Scorsese after cinema

My third argument with respect to the function of commercials in the film, as a critique of representation, connects them thus to the other metacinematic flourishes outlined above: Belfort's speeches and Scorsese's bag of tricks. I now want to turn to those techniques but not without a final word on the specific way in which commercials function in this regard. The commercials' succession suggests a critique of cinematic representation, its situating with respect to media specificity. Here some of the qualifications above can be useful: the documentary aspects of the commercial, the return of the lion as human libido. But the commercials also cue us in to how to watch the film, and this is especially so with the interrupted commercial, the "fucking infomercial" shown late in the film.

Throughout *The Wolf of Wall Street*, Belfort addresses his stockbrokers from a stage like a Vegas huckster, cracking obscene jokes, mimicking fellatio with the microphone (or hitting his head with it), wheedling and inspiring his team to be "telephone terrorists," threatening them with a vision of cut-rate loserdom, all in an effort to push them to make money, for themselves, but mostly for him. These speeches add another dimension of mediatized performance to the film, showing how much the 1990s era of penny stock pushing was as much about entertainment as finance capital. And like his direct addresses to the camera, or other voice-over moments, they blur the question of who is the audience: the salesmen, the cinema audience, or some combination of both. In a social remake of the "you talkin' to me?" speech in *Taxi Driver*, the film, in addressing us, in what is called *interpellating* us, makes us uncertain about our own identity. This address makes the film, in the video game cliché, *immersive*. Finally, in a key way, the speeches suggest the role that knowledge plays in the film. If Belfort is paranoid (as indicated in Winter's screenplay notes), and in this way like the taxi driver, Travis Bickle, this is a case, again, of *The Man Who Knew Too Much*.

This is the title of a key Hitchcock film (that he himself made twice, in 1934 and again in 1956), and I want to briefly discuss how knowledge is treated by Hitchcock as a way to understanding its different use in *The Wolf of Wall Street*. For Hitchcock, knowledge is a way to get power, but also to be punished. Men are constantly being punished or hunted down, and so on, for what they know (but do not know they know: like the Freudian unconscious). The man who knew too much (James Stewart's character) is on vacation in Morocco and learns of a plot to murder an ambassador in London. In this way he is like Stewart's character in *Rear Window* (1954: who suspects a murder but cannot act), or Henry Fonda's in *The Wrong Man* (1956: based on a true story, persecuted for an act he is innocent of), or Cary Grant's in *North by North West* (1959: mistaken for a fictitious spy, he is chased both by the Soviet other and also, amorously, by Eva Marie Saint's character, working for the US spy agency).

This figure of the man who knows too much is an exceedingly modernist notion of the subject, of what it is to be human, and poses a critique, evidently of the knowledge forms that came to be privileged in the postwar "information society." Its appearance in Scrosese's films as paranoia is another example of Lukács' theory of the pathological: thus the taxi driver and the coke-snorting stockbroker both see that "people are after him" but cannot decide who that is. Those stock "masculinity" figures show us how masculinity is so often in crisis. *The Wolf of Wall Street* resolves this contradiction by having characters who valorize *not* knowing: both Belfort, when he is "explaining" his crimes but stops, and, via negation, Donnie Azoff, when he brags how he knows how to make money. In the end, *The Wolf of Wall Street* is an anti-Hitchcock film, one that shows how you are punished (loses property, sent to jail) for not knowing enough. But even to entertain this thesis is to admit its opposite. Belfort has a skill that will allow him to bounce back, and so in the end he is not punished: he has a film about his life.

Voice-over redux

But what kind of film is it, and what is it saying about Belfort's life (even if not specifically, if it was showing a certain white male privilege in all its debauched glory)? As a Scorsese film, it consistently comments on that story, on its telling, with devices such as wipes, freeze-frames, extra-diegetic sound, and spot-on soundtrack clips that draw our attention to the filmic process.

The Wolf of Wall Street shares not a few of these qualities with *Goodfellas*, including not simply voice-overs, but more than one simultaneously. We see this in *Goodfellas*, when Karen and Henry tell their stories at the same time, and in *The Wolf of Wall Street* in two scenes: when Belfort is negotiating with a Swiss banker, and when he is flirting with his wife's aunt Emma. In both examples in *The Wolf of Wall Street*, the voice-overs end up as separate channels: addressed to, but unheard by, each other, they are only for the audience. Both film's doubling of the voice-over are in this regard akin to *The Departed*'s doubling of the informant or stool pigeon. These are formal gestures, which layer a technique both to exploit its story potential and as a mannerist filigree. In the doubled voice-overs in our film, the story potential is that here we are seeing Belfort out of his depth, with the European aristocracy: remember that Belfort calls his wife Duchess because of her aunt (in American cinema, European actors and accents are inevitably a code for old world elegance). The doubled voice-over does not accomplish the same work as in *Goodfellas*, where the technique promotes Karen Hill (Lorraine Bracco)'s role in the film. Rather, the voice-over is here more accurately *quadrupled*—or at least tripled—since we have both the aunt and the Swiss banker. The doubling or tripling of this device draws our attention to the voice-over itself *qua* technique, which is to say to the weirdness that we have a voice-over at all, more properly a feature of antiquated forms such as the hardboiled mystery or radio play.[4] But this tripling of the voice-over also offers a rejoinder to, or even a *clarification* of, the exuberance of the opening scene, when we see Belfort driving his sports car. A woman is fellating him, and, in a weird moment, Belfort tells us, via voice-over, to "put your dick back in your pants" because the woman is his wife. On one level, this is good old-fashioned male bonding: he assumes the viewer is a heterosexual male who is turned on by such a scene. But perhaps Belfort is talking to himself? Isn't putting your dick back into your pants what one does after such an act? We, at the beginning of the film, see (or hear and see, for this is about the role of sound and image) a nonmonolithic voice-over. A voice-over that betrays itself.

Equally self-reflexive is what the film does with Belfort's car. In the opening montage, we see a red sports car and the voice-over quickly comments that his car was *white*, like Don Johnson's in *Miami Vice*, and the car is suddenly white. Much later, Belfort attempts to drive the same car while rendered senseless by Qualuudes. In this protracted scene, Belfort is so incapacitated by drugs that he can only crawl to his car; he drives so slowly that other drivers honk at him as they pass. In the morning he is woken by the police who take him outside to see a wrecked car. We then see the drive home again, as it "actually" happened, complete with sideswipes of other vehicles, knocked over mailboxes, and the like. These are narrative intrusions of first a minor, then a major, key; the first, the car that changes color, is a mere flourish, while the second requires the sudden acquisition of viewerly skepticism (if one did not already possess such a skill). That both gestures involve a car is itself a comment, first on the mutability of these widespread commodities, and then on the desire to destroy them. Both scenes want us *not to trust the film*. Further, the second scene, in its repetition of the driving sequence, wants us not to trust our identification with a drunken, stoned, Belfort.

Adaptation and levitation

It will be remembered that Jameson aligns the very formal qualities of film with its ability to elicit our pleasure, drawing on Freud's comment that, in contrast to daydreams, which always bore us, with an artwork we are essentially bribed by aesthetic pleasure. We can test Jameson's thesis in the following way via the trope of adaptation, or how one medium treats or reworks another (keeping in mind that we have already argued that the film effectively destroys media in general). When we compare the same passage or incident in Belfort's memoir to its realization in Scorsese's film (which is, admittedly, a little cruel—a first-time author, one of the leading filmmakers of the twentieth century), well, there is no contest.[5] Where Belfort (as author) describes a domestic spat, he gets caught up in the name brands and cost of the décor in his bedroom ("five-hundred-dollar monogrammed Pratesi bath towel," and so forth), the film stages a conflict, always centered on Belfort as self-deluding hero, flexing his pecs and looking, his wife tells him, ridiculous.[6] But this comparison is not for the purpose of some moralistic Marxism that will deny the reader or viewer her (guilty) pleasure in the commodity. Consider another film starring Leonardo DiCaprio, *The Great Gatsby* (Baz Luhrmann, 2013), and the fantastic scene where Gatsby throws his shirts onto his bed, for Daisy to luxuriate in. Now, while the scene in the film does manage to bring out a visual pleasure (fore-pleasure?) to this display of wanton commodification, it cannot stand up to F. Scott Fitzgerald's description, which states in no uncertain terms the traumatic effect the shirts have on Daisy, shirts, it will be remembered, that are "piled like bricks in stacks a dozen high," shirts that end up in a "soft rich heap," shirts with "stripes and scrolls and plaids in coral and apple-green and lavender and faint orange with monograms of Indian blue," shirts into which "Daisy bent her head … and began to cry stormily," a roiling cry of anguish one can image leaving great globules of snot and mucous, staining the ever-inadequate shirts, fabric, objects, things, that Gatsby acquires to compensate himself for his own inner loss.[7] Both of these examples affirm Jameson's axiom as to the importance of a difference in aesthetic value between book and film.

I argued above that these ways in which *The Wolf of Wall Street* engages in self-reflexive media can, in the end, be understood as a formal critique of finance capital, the film's putative object of study. Capitalism is not problematic merely because stockbrokers behave badly (a moral critique) but also because of its inherent lack of basis in reality. But such a reading, what I call the "laborist-substantialist" critique, we have already seen to be limited in its theoretical or political value. A final way to think about postmodernism in our film might be better followed by a more direct "application" of Jamesonian theory to Scorsese's film. In his postmodernism essay, Jameson discusses problems of space and the subject with two examples: the elevators and escalators (the "people-movers") in the Bonaventura hotel, and Michael Herr's description of riding in helicopters as a war correspondent in the Vietnam War. Conveniently enough, we have just such vehicles at hand in *The Wolf of Wall Street*. A helicopter is a natural enough toy for the superrich, it seems, and thus even Belfort's yacht has a landing pad (the helicopter falls off during the Mediterranean storm scene). And there is also a key elevator scene that illustrates the work hard/play hard dialectic of Stratton Oakmont. The two moments in which helicopters are important come, first of all, during the opening few minutes of the film, where we see a drunken Belfort try to land his chopper at his Long Island mansion. Then, when he is filming the infomercial, he exits a copter, into the waiting arms of the FBI. The crucial elevator scene comes when Stratton has a new building, and two employees "christen" the elevator with an act of oral sex—with a blowjob. The chopper and elevators, thus, are sites for affective intensities of the narcotic and libidinal—but also postmodern, we can be sure—varieties.

The Wolf of Wall Street's political unconscious

What is the unconscious of *The Wolf of Wall Street?* Jameson's Marxist version of psychoanalysis, it will be remembered, argues that a political interpretation will restore a film or novel's "unsaid," its *non-dit*, by way of bringing to the surface not only what cannot be said in the film or novel, but also *how* the text makes those things unsayable, the film's "structural limitation and ideological closure." I argue that there are certain key scenes in *The Wolf of Wall Street* in which such limitations and closures can be detected: the yacht storm, Belfort's references to the poor, and moments of scapegoating (Belfort's gay butler, a hapless employee cleaning his fish tank). The two scapegoating scenes are especially telling.

Bro-mophobia

Naomi, Belfort's second wife, the "Duchess of Bay Ridge," hires a gay butler, a luxury item according to Belfort. Naomi comes home unexpectedly to the butler cavorting naked with a dozen men. Money has also gone missing—$40,000 from the sock drawer, and Belfort and his friends confront the butler, work him over, hang him out the window, and turn him over to the police for further beatings. Not, however, before the butler has "outed" Azoff, who admits to going to gay clubs.

A few scenes later, on a day when Stratton Oakmont was preparing a new stock issue, Belfort spots a young broker (Thomas Middleditch) cleaning his goldfish bowl. This sends Belfort, and Donnie Azoff, into a tizzy. Azoff upbraids the employee: "On new issue day? On cocksuckin' motherfuckin' new issue day? This is what you do?" and proceeds to eat the goldfish. The broker is fired, as the other employees throw things at him, mocking him for his bow tie.

Both of these scenes are remarkable for the difficulty we have in determining exactly why the character must be scapegoated. Homophobia is undoubtedly present in the butler scene, but it also is undermined in two ways. By now (this is more than an hour into the film), we have seen any number of heterosexual scenes, and a great deal of (usually female) nudity. So, the quick shots of gay male sex are in a way of a piece with the film's ethos. As well, when the butler is confronted, he retorts that he saw Azoff "last month at the Lollipop Club." As other men in the room exchange glances, the butler argues that he is being confronted because he is gay, to which Azoff replies "You think this is because you're a fag? My cousin's a fucking faggot and I go on vacation with him and his boyfriend, I love fags." Now, we have already learned about Azoff's possibly incestuous marriage with his cousin (he must have some interesting cousins), but apparently these forms of deviance do not mark him as an outsider to the Stratton clan. The homophobia behind Belfort et al.'s beating of the gay butler is meta, or reflexive. Call it bromophobia, one will declare one's tolerance if it gives you the excuse to indulge in obscene language: *My cousin's a fucking faggot and I go on vacation with him and his boyfriend, I love fags.*

But there is also an unusual dynamic at work here: for if the butler is so rudely treated as a way to exorcise from the male compact that which is already in the male compact (which is to say, Azoff as a homosexual or bisexual), perhaps we should ask why Azoff himself is not ejected or excluded. Azoff is in some ways close to what Lee Edelman, in *No Future*, calls a *sinthomosexual*, or a queer character who embodies a lack of future (and therefore is a rebuke to the Utopian nature of the film's program—but not, perhaps, to what Jameson calls "disruptive futurity"). Edelman argues that in contemporary America, children, and what he calls "the fascism of the baby's face," hold a particularly odious grip on the imagination as a signal of capitalism's enduring permanence, and that, therefore, those who challenge such an ideology—whether "party hearty" queers or certain characters in films (he discusses Hitchcock's *North by Northwest* and *The Birds* [1963])— must be particularly marginalized. And this issue of children is applicable here, for when Belfort and Azoff first meet, Belfort asks him about his marriage to his cousin, wondering if Azoff isn't worried about possible birth defects in their children. Azoff then says, with a straight face, that he would just dump the kid in the country, "and let it go, you're free." And so it is all the more important for Azoff and the crew to eject the gay butler, *since they are already queer—or sinthomosexual— enough.* And given the importance Edelman ascribes to a scene in *North by Northwest* where a character steps on Roger

Thornhill's (Cary Grant's) fingers while he clings to the edge of Mount Rushmore, there is perhaps a little repetition going on when Belfort's crew dangle the butler over the balcony.

The Stratton broker who is rudely fired on an IPO day is another case of what appears to be someone doing what he is supposed to. In the memoir's telling of this incident, Belfort notes that Stratton employees had "iguanas, ferrets, gerbils, parakeets, turtles, snakes, mongooses."[8] And the excessive work hard/play hard ethos of the firm, of the film, has, again, already been established. My suggestion here, with both of these scenes, then, is that the film is producing an immanent critique of its own ideology, a structural critique which is in effect empty of content.

What do I mean by this? In both scenes, the expelled character embodies in an unremarkable way what is otherwise utterly typical of the film and its ideology: excessive sexual appetites in the case of the butler, and a blending of private desires (the pet) in the workplace in the case of the bowtied broker. (Even the bowtie is hardly remarkable in the context of Azoff's wannabe-WASP sweaters tied over the shoulder.) In both cases, what is expelled is the film's or its ideology's own interiority, its own paradigm.

The film excludes itself

There are two other instances of the film incorporating or encountering an outside: the scene where Belfort's yacht is destroyed in a Mediterranean storm, and his speech where he inspires his brokers with the specter of poverty. The yacht storm takes place late in the film, when Belfort, learning that Naomi's British aunt has passed away, panics because she is the nominal owner of his Swiss millions. In a complicated effort to evade passport controls and file fraudulent documents in Switzerland, he orders his yacht captain to take them into a storm. The scene is played as much for laughs as danger— Belfort is more concerned with making sure he is high on

Quaaludes—and when they are rescued by the Italian navy, the final scene is more disco than *Poseidon*.

Belfort's speech—on the occasion of the Steve Madden IPO—at first glance seems equally innocuous. It is worth quoting, however:

> Let me tell you something. There is no nobility in poverty. I have been a rich man and I have been a poor man, and I choose rich every fucking time…If anyone here thinks I'm superficial, or materialistic, go get a job at fuckin' McDonalds, cause that's where you fuckin' belong. But before you depart this room full of winners, I want you to take a good look at the person next to you, go on. Because sometime in the not-so-distant future, you're going to be pulling up to a red light in your beat-up old fuckin' Pinto, and that person's going to be pulling up right along side of you, in their brand-new Porsche, with their beautiful wife by their side, who's got big voluptuous tits, and who are you gonna be sitting next to? Some disgusting wildebeest with three days of razor stubble, in a sleeveless mumu, crammed in next to you in a carload full of groceries from fuckin' Price Club. That's who you're going to be sitting next to. So you listen to me and you listen well. Are you behind on your credit card bills? Good! Pick up the phone and start dialing. Is your landlord ready to evict you? Good! Pick up the phone and start dialing. Does your girlfriend think you're a fuckin' worthless loser? Good! Pick up the phone and start dialing. I want you to deal with your problems by becoming rich!

The manifest content, and the purpose, of the speech is clear: to motivate the sales team to push Steve Madden stock. But its logic is less clear. First, the bugbear that working at McDonald's (let us say fast-food chains) is a less noble occupation (this comes up again during a mock ad for Jordan Belfort's Straight Line). Then, the caricature of—let's call it social inequality, since the film has already floated that idea with its invocation of the "1 percent." So, we have the nightmare of driving a

Pinto, with an unattractive wife, kids, and discount groceries. Or, the fantasy of driving a Porsche, and a looker of a wife. This contrast is an indication of another "outside" to the logic of the film: the outside of ugly people, the poor, with beater cars, forced to shop at a warehouse store.

But the cinematic *presentation* of this "outside" may also indicate another dynamic at work in the question of the film's *non-dit*. Watching a film is not merely to see static symbols offered for the viewer's decoding. This may be one of the major myths that surround political or Marxist film criticism, that it finds the corporate villain, the heroic worker, and then considers its work done. Rather, as Jameson makes clear in *The Political Unconscious*, interpretation is a way of finding those moments where a film or novel fails, where it covers up or represses its historical reality. So, it is not merely that the speech depicts the poor in a mocking, offensive manner (centered in particular on women's bodies). Rather, the point of a Jamesonian interpretation is to ask why should that caricature be necessary to the film? Why, in particular, does this speech summon the specter of someone *leaving* Stratton Oakmont? Why is Belfort worried that "anyone here thinks I'm superficial, or materialistic?"

Here, I suggest, we have the same logic as with the scapegoating of the gay butler and the bowtied broker (the scene with that broker comes immediately before the Price Club speech): the moralistic (those with a critique of social inequality) must be expelled, and not only because that critique is a threat to Stratton Oakmont (to capitalism), *but also because that critique comes from within Stratton Oakmont*. That critique, the critique of social inequality, is the ORIGIN of the firm, with its desire to rip off the "1 percent." That is the true *non-dit*, the "political unconscious," of *The Wolf of Wall Street*: that the origins of capitalism, or its secret heart, lie in a critique of a previous social inequality. The truth here is conceptual rather than historical: it is not so much that the film is providing a history of capitalism (its origins in a struggle against feudalism, as argued by Marx and Engels in *The Communist Manifesto*) or even a handbook for how it works (it knows we do not know). Rather, like Donnie

Azoff declaring he is smart because he's worried he is not, the Belfort conjures up (and symbolically ejects) the specter of a moralistic critic because that critic is—himself.

Wall Street as Utopia!

One of the major arguments in the previous chapter lay in Jameson's counterintuitive thesis that all cultural objects—films, television shows, books, songs—contain a Utopian kernel or truth or criticism of our contemporary society. How does this work with *The Wolf of Wall Street?* I would say that this plays out in the following ways: first, in terms of the film's most objectionable content—its displays of misogyny, its heteronormativity and white privilege, its disgusting parade of wealth and capitalistic excess. Then, in the film's very embrace of the work hard/play hard ethos, not simply is the film invested in such a dialectic, but it sees no distinction, and so too the role of crime in the film. At one level, this is a gangster film masquerading as a Wall Street film, and at another level, the difference, in a Blochian sense, is nonexistent. Finally, the film's great themes can be found in terms of what Jameson describes as Utopian spatiality, or the enclave: both the urban and suburban spaces of Manhattan and New York/Long Island, and in the office space (but also the garage) as a lived environment, as a work place.

Hope and envy

The notion of Utopia, or the Utopian impulse, has been a constant in Jameson's writings but especially in its strongest form, the argument that *all* ideological or cultural productions contain some germ of a Utopian impulse. This is Bloch's most fundamental argument: that all cultural production is Utopian in an ontological sense (because in writing a poem or making a film we are engaged in a project) but also in specific and generic senses (thus, the musical form of a sonata is an engagement with time, the architectural form of a cupola works with space).

As argued earlier, a film's Utopian strategy has to do with how cultural production is located historically, and that any historical present will contain residues of the past. How do we come to grips with the misogyny to be found in *The Wolf of Wall Street*—the way that women's bodies are on display for the audience but also the limited roles they play in the film's story and development (even and up to and including what may be Belfort's rape of his wife)? Such patriarchal actions seem out of place in a film set in the 1990s, and yet are evidently the residue of another era. This would be a way in which to consider, then, *all* of the film's objectionable content, from the shaving of a female employee's head to the stock market-like grading of different prostitutes, the dwarf-tossing, the homophobia both verbal and rather more than gay bashing but almost homocide, and (why not?) the treatment of animals with the "humiliation" of dressing a chimpanzee up in a miniature business suit. Just how are such actions in the film a matter of a Utopian impulse?

Consider one scene, when a female broker is portrayed having her head shaved for $10,000. Describing the progression from masquerade to terror in 1930s Germany, Bloch describes how "the Jews with cut-off trousers and with witty placards around their necks, the Jewish sweethearts with shorn heads in the train triggered salvos of laughter, before they triggered different salvos," and this is not far removed, in his analysis from an economic metaphor of Wall Street crashes as a deterrent to crime.[9] For Bloch, the difference between crime and finance is as imaginary as it is for Freud between a daydream and a work of art. But this is also to remind us of the role of envy in any Utopian endeavor (which can then be added as another cause for the expelled characters discussed above).

If *The Wolf of Wall Street* holds onto residual or outmoded attitudes, such as homophobia or misogyny, it is possible to detect in the film some "emergent" structures, which may simply be alternative to the dominant forms, or indicative of the coming into being of a new class, a new hope in Bloch's sense. Certainly, we can see that Belfort's entire project is to battle it out against the dominant stock brokers (as when he offers to tell the FBI agent about the goings-on of the most prestigious firms, Goldman Sachs, Lehmann Brothers, Merrill), in this sense the Utopian impulse of *The Wolf of Wall Street*. And there is some complicated relationship between this hint of nefarious goings-on that occurred on a much larger scope (and which do not appear in the memoir, which was published before the financial crisis, in 2007) and the question of the representability of technology.

Don't work or play

Like the contradiction of sex and the economic that bedevils any analysis of our film (remembering that Belfort says the drug he is really addicted to is money), the work hard/play hard ideologeme mystifies with its looping causality: is playing hard our reward for working hard (and thus leisure is merely an extension of capitalist domination), or is working hard *actually its own reward?* We have work, perhaps as a Utopian project, then, in our film as well. Perhaps one of the mystificatory— which is to say *ideological*—projects of *The Wolf of Wall Street* is precisely its imagining of such hard workers—after all, as Jameson asks, isn't the point of a socialist revolution to eliminate or at least to reduce the amount of work one has to do? Who wants to work hard all the time?

One way to tackle this dilemma is to think of the difference between alienated and unalienated labor—work, to put it crudely, that you enjoy (and don't get exploited economically or psychologically) versus work that you do not enjoy (that is dangerous, soul-sucking). Our conceptions of work are often so complicated by these paradoxes—thus I envy my teenaged son for sleeping in on the weekends—for being a slacker—and I worry that immigrants are taking jobs away—a self-contradictory attitude best explained, as Jameson does drawing on Žižek, by the idea of the other "stealing" my *jouissance*. And what *that* means is that I really don't like my own enjoyment or *jouissance*—I hate my job, so I'm worried someone is going to steal it, or doesn't have to work, or whatever. These intensities of anxiety and rage are also mobilized in *The Wolf of Wall Street*, when, as we have already seen, Belmont warns his salesmen about the "losers" sitting in a Pinto with groceries from a discount store, or mocks the FBI agent "sweating his balls" as he rides the subway home.

But this mention of the FBI agent reminds us again that there is crime afoot here, and it is worth exploring the Utopian dimensions of such activity. Here I want to return to the way Belfort assembles his "crew," and the cinematic means employed in the service of this effort. I have already commented upon the collectivity being allegorized here, and we can add to this a notion of what Jameson calls the "allegory of production." Importantly, not only is the sequence shown twice (one of a number of "doublings" in the film, from the voice-overs to the car sequences), but we are also confronted with the homogeneity of the crew: they are mostly white-ethnic Long Islander males—Italian, Jewish, but also the Asian-American, Chester Ming, inevitably referred to as a "Chinaman."

Think of how other crime films deal with racial or ethnic identity. In the two versions of *The Taking of Pelham One Two Three* (Joseph Sargent, 1974, and Tony Scott, 2009) we see a kind of "progress"—Walter Matthau's character in the first is played by Denzel Washington in the second. But also, remember our discussion of color—from Jameson on the reification of the visual to the switched colors of Belfort's Ferrari. In *The Taking of Pelham One Two Three*, the characters' color identities in the first film—Mister Blue, Green, Gray, Brown—can be seen as a compensation for their *lack of color*—or at least for their unbearable whiteness. This strategy is mobilized more knowingly in *Reservoir Dogs*, arguably. So, we can interpret the crew of brokers in *The Wolf of Wall Street*—for all their emerging from criminal petty-capitalist class—or perhaps *because* of that provenance, as such a Utopian projection, a Utopia in the problematic sense that their lack of racial diversity is a kind of universalism of the particular. As Long Island ethnic males, they stand in for all of us.

Thieves in a heist picture are not a multicultural representation of some mythic and ideal America (a false universalism, already present in the screenplay for *The Wolf of Wall Street*) but instead project a universalism by dint of their collective project. The doubling of the crew scene then (restaurant kibitzing followed by workplace mug shots) accomplishes that collectivity via cinematic technique that is both meta and post-cinema, this last in the sense that such scenes are tailor-made for going viral on social media or YouTube (and, indeed, may be mimicking such a genre).

The Long Island shed

Jameson asserts, following Roland Barthes, that the quintessential place of the Utopian impulse can be found in "the experience everyday life," where individual and collective times find their coexistence. This space or time-space is in the film to be found most assuredly in the workplace, which then turns out to be not only the place where brokers yell into phones and make deals and cheer on their boss, but also watch naked marching bands and dwarf-tossing and fornicate with prostitutes. But we will want to dig a little further, or remember the film a little more accurately, for as key to Belfort's early narrative as his assembling of a crew is the site for his first office: an auto body shop. And here we have, yet again, another doubling.

We will remember that Jameson's Utopian thinkers and tinkerers are both located spatially (in a workshop or a garage) and, in their collectivity, resemble the misfits and mutts who populate the heist picture (or its dialectical television form, *Wire*, where the criminals and the police reflect each other narratively). So too, when Belfort makes his first sale in the

Long Island strip plaza, he is pitching Aerotyne, a technology company, and we see a still photo of a backyard shed or garage with the sign "Aerotyne Ind." Here the Utopian shed of the inventor is matched by the Utopian garage of the start-up investors (the hucksters, the scam artists).

In addition, the brokers' office is a form of that important Utopian space that is the *enclave*—the space, like Thomas More's island in *Utopia*, that somehow is set off from society, offering a laboratory-like place to get it right. In describing this spatiality, Jameson argues that every sector of the postmodern economy spins out its own subsectors, and so the Utopian space is an isolated enclave in the real world of the social, a temporary or peripheral spatial moment that resists the overall tendencies of capitalism. And this is precisely how Belmont's firm is portrayed in the film—starting, especially, in that strip mall in Long Island (or as Public Enemy name it, "Strong Island"), a "boiler room" operation of hard sell and an all-too proximate (and loud) toilet. Spatiality lives a secret under-life in *The Wolf of Wall Street*. For instance, when Belmont's wife, the so-called "Duchess of Bay Ridge," mentions off-handedly the slang expression for that Brooklyn neighborhood's bridge, the Verrazano–Narrows Bridge, the "Guinea gangplank," the phrase signals again such a Utopian enclave or space.

The film displays an astonishing range in terms of space: sometimes it is extremely specific, using dialogue or scenic clues to signal New York neighborhoods (Bay Ridge: the "Guinea Gulch"); other times, it moves around as easily as capital flows do the globe, mashing up place names, locations, and countries (Venice, Italy; Venice, California). Note, also, how the spaces of the film are sometimes conveyed with establishing shots (of Belfort's mansion on Long Island's "Gold Coast"—a shot that would have been made with a helicopter similar to the one Belfort drunkenly crashes) and sometimes with time-lapse filming (as Belfort's business grows in an old auto repair shop). Thinking about the film spatially will help us to detect its inner utopian impulse, and so we can think about the film in terms of its "cognitive mapping" of New York (a perennial Scorsese strategy), the space of the brokerage itself (already characterized as postmodern), and how the film's hypermasculine subject, the "bro," works spatially. These spatial aspects of the film then help us in the interpretation of Utopia in terms of the film's origins: for Belfort describes himself, in his memoir, as "a precocious young banker, who'd created my own self-contained universe out on Long island, where normal behavior no longer applied"[10].

Islands and gangplanks

Scorsese is often characterized, along with Woody Allen and Spike Lee, as the quintessential New York filmmaker: from *Mean Streets* and *Taxi Driver* to *Goodfellas*, *The Age of Innocence*, and *Gangs of New York* (2002), he has depicted the city in different historical periods, but especially in the past forty years, from the crisis-ridden 1970s to the gentrified 1990s. A patch of dialogue at Belfort and Naomi's first date is key for establishing spatiality in this film:

JORDAN: So, Bay Ridge. That's near Staten Island, right?
NAOMI: Brooklyn, across the Verrazano Bridge.
JORDAN: *Saturday Night Fever* territory.
NAOMI: That's right. "Guinea gulch." We call the Verrazano Bridge the "Guinea Gangplank."

Learning that Naomi has an English aunt, Belfort will christen Naomi "the Duchess of Bay Ridge," a moniker that brings together two spaces—an ethnic enclave, and Britain. Naming is an important way in which space is mobilized in the film: the yacht Belfort buys for their wedding is the *Naomi*, when he has said the name of prostitute in his sleep (improbably, Venice), Belfort tries (unsuccessfully) to argue he was thinking of investing in a condo in Venice, California.

Naming also functions more generally, both with the company, whose name, Stratton Oakmont, is designed to suggest old money brokerage firms, and Belfort himself, who, after being called the "Wolf of Wall Street" in a *Forbes* article, takes on that name, being called "Wolfie" by his friends and employees, and even using it as a "safe word" when playing with the prostitute. But even the moniker "Guinea gangplank" seems to align with a Jamesonian sense of Utopian space: this term for the Verrazano Bridge derives from the bridge's connection to Staten Island, to which borough Italian-Americans moved after the bridge opened in 1964. The slang term thus denotes movement out of an ethnic enclave.

The scene is about more than Belfort naming Naomi: it is an attempt on the part of the film to locate the glittery world of its diegesis in a real, ethnic New York. To be sure, this can be seen as an *auteurist* tic of Scorsese's. But the gesture also has to do with, I would argue, the way space is both mobilized and fixed in the film. To put it crudely, when Belfort stays in one place or space, he is safe (or thinks he is); when he moves, he is in trouble.

Think of the scenes where he takes his friends to Vegas for his bachelor party, or flies to Europe to set up a money laundering scheme, or heads into a storm in his yacht in the Mediterranean: these are all disasters, caused not a little by his drug use, but also indicating the costs of moving money and bodies across space. But when Belfort stays in one place, when he finds a Long Island auto body shop, when he is in his enclave, then he succeeds. The ultimate point (whether it is origin or goal) for this progression or dialectic is perhaps the scene where Naomi is teasing Belfort with her legs open, unwittingly filmed by their security camera and watched by his security guards Rocco and Rocco. Naomi thinks she is maliciously flirting with Belfort—offering him her sex but also denying it to him. But that space is on display to the security guards, who stand in for the viewer. In this way, the spatiality of Utopia returns to Bloch's distortion of hope, and the enclave turns out to be a fantasy.

Conclusion

Trailer for *Yeezus*

There is an Agatha Christie novel in which Poirot and Hastings attend a play, a play that is itself about a detective. Poirot later criticizes the play for its lack of veracity to his profession, to which Hastings retorts that he cannot engage in the proper Coleridgean "suspension of disbelief." His own occupation taints his critical faculties … This same problematic haunts any Marxist interpretation of a film about capitalism: so, too, do we think we understand this putative object of our study and praxis. So, too, are we in danger of ignoring the entertainment or aesthetic pleasures of the film. However, Jameson's argument has been that our proper object of study is not necessarily that object (which is to say, in this case, the film), but rather the categories and ideological presuppositions that we bring, consciously or not, to that study.

And so I would like to bring this book to a conclusion with a discussion not of the film itself, but one of the trailers for the film. Released in June 2013 (six months before the film's Christmas release), the trailer shows scenes from the film— Mark Hanna schooling Belfort, mayhem in the office and on the dance floor, the car switching colors, dwarf-tossing—to the thudding sound of Kanye West's "Black Skinhead." Now, in a 1997 essay on "Culture and Finance Capital," Jameson argues, following Giovanni Arrighi's *The Long Twentieth Century*, that speculation, the turn to finance capital, is a sign of the end of a cycle, is "the way in which capitalism now reacts to and compensates for the closing of its productive moment."[1] This historical period extends to our own—the essay was published during the heyday of Belfort's run on Wall Street—and the cultural form that Jameson seizes on is the movie trailer. Like derivatives and other financial instruments, he remarks, they are fully autonomous (he will later say "singular") units: one no longer need see the actual film being advertised, for, in a manner reminiscent of the "incentive bonuses" offered by artworks in general, the trailers seem to boil down the film to its essentials, its shots or highlights as a kind of Platonic ideal of the film, not bothering with plot or narrative causality.

As if to confirm Jameson's intuition, Scorsese had already declared that his method, in filming *Goodfellas*, was to make it "move as fast as a trailer … to do it as if it was one long trailer."[2] But Scorsese is talking about speed, and Jameson is talking about leaving things out; what we discover with the "Black Skinhead" trailer is that, instead, the trailer adds something, for Kanye West's song is nowhere in the final film. Now, as Jameson notes, the more skillful trailers mislead us about a film, to set up expectations that are spectacularly demolished when we see the film. Such a distortion that, industry friends tell me, there are companies that specialize in trailers which intentionally sabotage the film's marketing. In the case of *The Wolf of Wall Street*, the cynical use of a hot track (the trailer was released online the same week West's album *Yeezus* was released) unwittingly points to the film's *non-dit*, its noninterest in non-whites.

Doubles

But a situating of our film in relation to Jameson's theory of finance capital can serve as a way in to what will be the conclusion to this study, in which I hope to make the argument that if, as Jameson opines, the Utopian project is in the end about the production of an unresolved contradiction or paradox, then perhaps this film, in its pursuit of a capitalism without any things (without the money that is so cumbersome), finds its own cause, or indeed *the* cause of the Scorsese canon: finance capital as the determinant of postmodern cinema. To unpack this assertion, it is necessary first of all to track what I have already remarked on a few times in the past pages: the plethora of figural doubling that goes on in the film, the dialectics (the Platonic ideal of doubling) of voice-overs, filmic cars, *fugazi/fugazy*, and the like; then, to bring back into our analysis what was shockingly neglected from my earlier discussion of the "political unconscious" of the film, which is to say, Jameson's three levels of interpretative analysis.

A catalog of the doubles in *The Wolf of Wall Street* includes, then:

- how the technique of the voice-over is doubled from Belfort's voice-over to, first, the Swiss banker's, and then also Naomi's aunt Emma's;

- the shed or garage in which Aerotyne industries is located, and the garage in which Belfort starts his business;

- the Ferrari that switches colors in the opening scene (and so is actually two different cars);

- the two scenes in which we see Belfort drive the Ferrari home, the first time successfully, the second with a series of crashes;

- the two security guards both named Rocco;

- the two pronunciations of *fugazi/fugazy* in the scene between Belfort and Hanna;

- the forms of TV commercials, both invented (Stratton Oakmont, Straight Line) and real (Steve Madden shoes, Benihana restaurants);

- the two scenes where Belfort introduces/assembles his crew of salesmen, first in the restaurant, then in the office;

- the two speeches in which Belfort addresses the camera directly, in both cases admitting that he does not know (and we do not need to know) how finance capitalism works (which then suggests the philosophical double of knowing/not knowing).

To this catalog we can then add interpretive doublings (for now our argument can reconstruct the "origins" of a dialectical reading of the film and find them in the film itself—but these doubles will now extend beyond Scorsese's film):

- cognitive mapping, as when Jameson remarks of that the network of telephone cables in *Three Days of the Condor* represents a paranoid conspiracy, a totality;

- the work hard/play hard dyad (and so the office is also a pleasure dome, and even domestic spaces are work spaces for the Rocco guards);

- the doubled informant trope in other films, including Scorsese's *The Departed*;

- the double or doublet of crime and finance;

- Utopian hope and envy;

- surface and depth (or the symptomatic: but also the doubled form in which Jameson's critics engage these tropes via literature and then film, as if a critical form of adaptation, which is then itself a doubling);

- pastiche and parody (both of which are themselves forms of doubling);

- cinematic repetition (thus the voice-over doubling repeats a Scorsesean trick from *Goodfellas*; which itself as a film was a "return" to the gangster motifs

of *Mean Streets*; and then forms of adaptation and
the sequel, including *The Departed* as a remake of
Internal Affairs).

But this last list threatens to take over this entire book, for a
dialectical film criticism will rely precisely on the thesis that
there is to be found in any work of cinema, in any movie, a
struggle for meaning, a struggle that is interpretive but also
ontological. The dialectic is a doubling in the sense that the
antithesis of any argument (or its instantiation in the world)
relies to some degree on its predecessor. And here doubling
and dialectics have to encounter other forms of dualisms, from
binary oppositions to antinomies: terms that are opposed to
each other and yet secretly draw on one another (as in the
binary, which poststructuralism did so much to dismantle) and
terms that are in some way thought to be mutually exclusive
(the antinomy then is the root cause of the semiotic rectangle
introduced in the discussion of class, above). But doubling
is also a figure to be found in the hope-filled project that is
finance capital (and its double, gambling), as in the phrase
"double your money."

Scorsese's doubles

It may be worthwhile to linger a bit longer with these two
lists of doubles, and see what they can provide. The technical
doublings that take place in the film—the voice-overs, the two
car tricks, the doubled crew scenes, the doubled speeches to the
camera (but also the two Roccos)—are all of a piece with the
film's postmodernism, they are there so that we "do not trust
our eyes" (or ears)—and even, in the case of the two addresses
to the camera, we do not trust our own cynicism. In some
secret way they accomplish two things, I would argue: first,
they undermine the veracity/authority of Belfort as the center
of the film; second, they are a thesis with respect to an analogy

between representation and finance capital (nailed, as it were, by the *fugazi/fugazy* discussion). Now this thesis (that finance capital deals with what Mark Hanna calls "fairy dust" just as a postmodern film reveals the artifice of its construction) is, as I have argued, faulty, in terms of how it ignores the exploitation and material basis of finance under the guise of its "laborist-substantialist" fallacy. Which is to ask: what is the double of the fairy dust? Is it, as I argued at this book's outset, money itself, money as an object that is then taped to a woman's breasts, trundled across airport floors in roll-on luggage, flung onto a bed for Belfort and Naomi to make love on, rolled-up to snort coke with, dumped in a parking lot out of a briefcase, dumped onto Brad's body along with a couple of naked girls?

Are these "money shots," to which we should add the ultimate money shot, perhaps first seen in Brian De Palma's *Scarface* (1983), but also in *The Wolf of Wall Street*: money being counted in an automatic machine? Like the plot points with which the materiality of money trips up our heroes (money laundering and the like), the automatic money counting machine denotes the thingness of money which itself can only be an analogy for the world that the finance capitalists, the "wolves," are trying to escape, even as, caught in their own contradiction, they retreat into the enclave.

The repetition of scenes—the two crew scenes, speeches, car scenes—pose another kind of hermeneutic puzzle, one suggested first of all by my substituting "repetition" for "doubling." The logics here of doubling, repetition, and substitution, then, are those of the commodity, of reification (more to do with things, again). Just as the Ferrari as a commodity itself is a double (when Belfort "corrects" the color in the early scene he tells us his car was "like the one Don Johnson drove in *Miami Vice*"), so too are all commodities: they are always, like a stunt double, a stand-in. But not a stand-in for a Platonic ideal, or even for the putative star of the picture.

Or, rather, perhaps, the Platonic idea of the commodity form itself—but in a media sense, for, as a film made in the digital present, the scene is now less a narrative seme than a freefloating object which can reappear on YouTube. The repeated or doubled scenes, then, are Scorsese's own remakes, as if he were a young filmmaker, hungry, grabbing a scene from his own movie and offering a different version. The logic of this is apparent if we compare these two different kinds of doubled scenes. The two car scenes, as noted above, establish a postmodern critique of representation, telegraphing, or short circuiting to the Jamesonian argument that such cinematic tricks are of a piece with late capitalism. That is, they instruct us not to trust the movie, just as we should not trust Wall Street. The two speeches then reflect on that lack of trust: now, with Belfort telling us he knows we do not know, should we trust that he even knows that? And then the two crew scenes are almost alternative takes, as if Scorsese cannot decide whether to indulge in a restaurant scene of camaraderie and kibitzing, or a more postmodern stand and deliver. What kind of doubling joins them? A modernist uncanny (didn't I just see this scene? with its postmodern version of wondering if the DVD has skipped)? An antinomy—are they mutually exclusive? A binary opposition—does the second scene bring out what was neglected or obscured in the first?

Jameson's doubles

Turning to the interpretive doubles, it is apparent first of all how some of them join the first list as forms or motifs of postmodernism: pastiche and parody, cinematic repetition (remakes and adaptation, the doubled informant), and also, I will argue, the dyad of surface and depth encountered in Jameson's critics. Other interpretive doubles belong more properly to a Marxist–Utopian critique: cognitive mapping, the work hard/play hard duality, the linkage of crime and finance, Blochian hope and envy, but also, smuggled in from the first list, the doubled sheds or garages (which motifs, probably not intended by Scorsese, thus are part of the film's political unconscious). Pastiche and parody are the hinge on which modernism/postmodernism are to be distinguished, Jameson argues in his postmodernism essay.

While the satiric impulse of parody has not disappeared from contemporary culture, a useful barometer of these two terms can be seen in the role the invented commercials play in the film: the opening Stratton Oakmont advert is played perfectly straight, and its inadequacy to the lunacy of Wall Street is only apparent in juxtaposition to the carnivalesque mayhem that follows. The notion of a doubled informant can be returned to profitably here, for even as that is one found elsewhere in Scorsese's films, it is worth remembering that the informant is *already* a double, a double agent. And then when Belfort refuses to go through with his deception of his friends (even as he is eating sushi with Azoff, he places a note on the table warning Azoff that he, Belfort, is wearing a wire), he has in effect "flipped" himself (to use the jargon of spy thrillers)—like the doubled and tripled voice-overs, he is now a triple agent, giving away his secret to his crew even as he pretends to betray them. This short moment in the film then brings together a few of the themes of this book: class solidarity, dialectics, and perhaps even the political unconscious.

The dyad of surface and depth is another form of doubling. Now, for Jameson, postmodernism proper signals the end of a kind of modernist hermeneutics of depth, be that found in the dialectics of essence and appearance, the Freudian unconscious, existential authenticity and *mauvaise foi*, or the semiotics of signifier and signified. This is no doubt startling to his "surface reading" and "post-theory" critics, who mistake what they see as the symptomatic program in Jameson for a belief in something lying under the surface. But Jameson's political unconscious is not the Freudian unconscious of the individual's repression, as I argued earlier: rather, properly (or fitfully) Lacanian, it is social, and so even the notion of an "outside" (as in to whence what cannot be tolerated in an ideological system is ejected) is only metaphorical, and not even that.

But it should be admitted that at various times, Jameson does entertain the possibility or necessity for interpretation of what is not hidden, what is on the surface—as we have already seen in his distinction between the Utopian impulse and the program, and as I have argued via the allegory of Hitchcock's *Rear Window*. So, what of the more Marxist or Blochian– Utopian motifs of doubling unearthed in this project—the doubled sheds, work hard/play hard, crime and finance, hope and envy, and cognitive mapping? The garage or shed that we glimpse briefly as the work site for Aerotyne (and we have to acknowledge the filmic qualities at work here: it is a still photo, so, again, we have a kind of media rivalry) is offered, in the film, as the "truth" of what Belfort is selling over the phone. While he is promoting the firm as a cutting-edge tech company with a patent about to make a lot of money, "in reality," the film suggests, it is only a backyard shed. And yet the *Utopian* truth of the scene—of the film—is that it is precisely in such humble surrounds or spaces that one finds Jameson's tinkerers and crackpots, the formulators of plans and schemes, who embody the Utopian impulse. And this is verified by the film itself, when, a few minutes later, Belfort and Azoff find an old auto body shop for their first office space. The truth, then, is that Belfort was not lying when he talked up Aerotyne, for in reality he was describing the Utopian longing that lay at the heart of his own enterprise.

The other dyads of work/play hard, hope and envy, crime and finance, are what we should view as dialectics, with the proviso that the dialectic has triumphed over other kinds of dualities, over the binary opposition and the antinomy. The dialectic of work and play is then also a matter of a binary, for the hard work demanded of stock brokers in late capitalism depends, the film argues, on their debauchery, on their degenerate habits of drugs and prostitution. And just as the firm itself is a Utopian enclave of hope—both selling it and believing in it—so too what motivates or protects that hope, that enclave, is both vicious envy or fear (the anxiety of ending up a Price Club member, which translates into the film's lamentable politics with respect to women, small people, and homosexuals) and also a logic or practice of exclusion: the gay butler, the bow-tied broker, and, eventually, Brad.

Wolf's doubles

What does the film offer us by way of cognitive mapping? Is it to be found in its affect, in the drug-fuelled paranoia? Or in its movement, its geography of money laundering and Vegas trips and helicopters and elevators? Or is it, again, what is on the surface: the selling of stocks itself, or, to be meta, the selling of the selling of stocks, for we should not let the earlier discussion of the voice-over to neglect Scorsese's other innovation in that regard: the direct address to the camera. For the voice-over is itself already a kind of doubling, a sound form unlike diegetic dialogue but also unlike acousmatic sound, in that we in the audience know (or think we know) who is addressing us. When Belfort addresses us directly, "breaking the fourth wall" as it used to be called, is this not a "voice-through" that wall? Perhaps, Belfort's voice itself, in dialogue, in voice-over, in direct address (to his sales team, to us) is the cognitive map of the film.

In his "Culture and Finance Capital" essay, Jameson entertains the proposition, not unlike those of the surface critics and post-theorists, that since the 1980s period of neoliberal deregulation "the motivations behind ideology no longer seem to need an elaborate machinery of decoding and hermeneutic reinterpretation…the guiding thread of all contemporary politics seems much easier to grasp, namely, that the rich want their taxes lowered." And yet, even if this is so, he adds, "we also face more objective problems about money itself" (256). It is therefore worthwhile to test this proposition by applying the most "elaborate machinery" in Jameson's shed or workshop, his theory of the three hermeneutic levels developed in *The Political Unconscious*, to help us bring to a close our understanding of the "objective problems about money" in *The Wolf of Wall Street*.

The Wolf's hermeneutics

Remember that Jameson argues the three levels all have their own form of cultural text or object: at the first level, we have the film itself, at the second, its ideologemes generated via a discursive struggle, and at the third, the form or medium or genre (so, here, film itself as narrative, and perhaps our perennial question of gangster versus finance film). At the first level, we have to think of our film in terms of what it does, *qua* symbolic act, and here we can return to the question of the Utopian mission, or the film's generation of an unresolved paradox or contradiction (keeping in mind Lévi-Strauss's "imaginary resolution of a real contradiction"). The contradiction, then, may lie in that problem of money, of the materiality of money, of the Utopian desire to make money without having to have the stuff. In this sense it engages with the everyday history of the newspapers and politics, of Occupy Wall Street and the financial crisis.

At a second level, the film is engaged in a struggle with other discourses, from Scorsese's own canon (hence my discussion of *Mean Streets*, *Goodfellas*, and even *The King of Comedy* earlier) but also contemporary American cinema and television. Out of that struggle we can see the importance of the ideologeme of the gangster, which for Scorsese embodies all of the contradictions of American life (his sequence on the American gangster film in his history of cinema is instructive in this regard). The character Brad has wandered into *The Wolf of Wall Street* as if from being an extra in *Goodfellas* or *The Sopranos* (it is no accident that the screenwriter for *The Wolf of Wall Street*, Terence Winter, also wrote for the TV series *The Sopranos* and *Boardwalk Empire*); like the gay butler, who is too much like Azoff to be allowed to stay in the film, Brad's gangsterishness makes him too dangerous to keep around.

The third level, then, of our analysis, takes us to genre and medium, to the gangster picture and film itself, and now we are engaging with history in its broadest forms. Now the film has found for Scorsese's canon, indeed for postmodern film itself, its absent cause, which is finance capital, or late capitalism. As a film, *The Wolf of Wall Street* doubles back on itself, continually testing its own theses: is the problem with capitalism the money that is involved, or is it how bodies are treated? Can a film represent the world out of which it emerges, and if so how? Jameson would argue that the answer to these questions can only be a political one, a Utopian one, an answer that suggests it is not only films that should be doing this questioning, this work, but all of us.

NOTES

Introduction

1   See Edward Jay Epstein, *Hollywood Economist: The Hidden Financial Reality behind the Movies* (Brooklyn: Melville House, 2010).
2   See Alberto Toscano and Jeff Kinkle, *Cartographies of the Absolute* (London: Zero Books, 2015), 172.

Chapter One

1   See Fredric Jameson, *Signatures of the Visible* (New York: Routledge, 1990), 19.
2   Nick Pinkerton, "Interview: Thelma Schoonmaker." *Film Comment*, March 21, 2014. http://www.filmcomment.com/blog/interview-thelma-schoonmaker/ (accessed February 1, 2016).
3   Jameson, *Signatures of the Visible*, 31.
4   See Sudeep Dasgupta, "Policing the People: Television Studies and the Problem of 'Quality'." *Necsus: European Journal of Media Studies*, Spring 2012. http://www.necsus-ejms.org/policing-the-people-television-studies-and-the-problem-of-quality-by-sudeep-dasgupta/ (accessed February 1, 2016).
5   In a review from the period, Karyn Kay asks "Why is DOG DAY AFTERNOON so popular in the cities? Perhaps because Lumet, with a vigilant eye to the new sexual consciousness (both real and professed) of the young, liberal urban audience, has taken the opportune cinematic and historical moment to spring a homosexual hero from the closet." "*Dog Day Afternoon*: Lumpen Lumet." *Jump Cut*, 10–11 (1976), 3. http://www.ejumpcut.org/archive/onlinessays/JC10-11folder/DogDayKay.html (accessed February 1, 2016). A full account of the historical

situation can also be viewed in the 2013 documentary on John Wojtowicz, *Dog* (Allison Berg, Frank Keraudren).

6   Jameson, *Signatures of the Visible*, 49.
7   Karl Marx, *Selected Writings*, ed. David McLellan (New York: Oxford University Press, 1977), 318.
8   Fredric Jameson, *The Geopolitical Aesthetic: Cinema and Space in the World System* (Bloomington: Indiana University Press, 1992), 14, 15.
9   See Andrew Blum, *Tubes: A Journey to the Center of the Internet* (New York: HarperCollins, 2012), Kindle loc. 2099.
10 See Jameson, *The Geopolitical Aesthetic*, 83-4n19, 76.
11 See George Kennan, "The Sources of Soviet Conduct." *Foreign Affairs* (July 1, 1947). https://www.foreignaffairs.com/articles/russian-federation/1947-07-01/sources-soviet-conduct (accessed February 2, 2016).
12 See Fredric Jameson, *The Political Unconscious: Narrative as a Socially Symbolic Act* (Ithaca: Cornell University Press, 1981), 49.
13 Jameson, *The Political Unconscious*, 63.
14 Ibid., 87.
15 Fredric Jameson, *Postmodernism, Or, the Cultural Logic of Late Capitalism* (Durham: Duke University Press, 1991), 44.
16 See Michael Herr, *Dispatches* (New York: Vintage, 1991), 25–26. Ctd. in Jameson, *Postmodernism*, 45.
17 Fredric Jameson, *The Cultural Turn: Selected Writings on the Postmodern, 1983–1998* (London: Verso, 1998), 8.
18 See Umberto Eco, "'Casablanca': Cult Movies and Intertextual Collage." *Substance* 14.2 (1985): 3–12.
19 See Jameson, *Postmodernism*, 20.
20 See Fredric Jameson, "The Aesthetics of Singularity." *New Left Review* 92 (March–April 2015), 101–132, 122.
21 See Ernst Bloch, *Principle of Hope*, Vol. 1 (Cambridge: MIT Press, 1996), 368.
22 See Fredric Jameson, *Archaeologies of the Future: The Desire Called Utopia and Other Science Fictions* (London: Verso, 2005), 3.
23 Freud, "The Creative Writer and Daydreaming," **SE 9**, 153. Ctd. *Archaeologies of the Future*, 47. Emphasis Freud's.
24 Bloch, *op. cit.*, 346.

25 See Fredric Jameson, "Realism and Utopia in *The Wire*."
    Criticism 52.3–4 (Summer–Fall 2010), 359–372, 364.

26 Jameson, *Archaeologies of the Future*, 233. See also Lee
    Edelman, *No Future: Queer Theory and the Death Drive*
    (Durham: Duke University Press, 2004).

27 See Karl Marx, *Capital*, Vol. III. Trans. David Fernbach
    (London: Penguin, 1991), 958–959.

28 Piketty discusses the "hypermeritocratic society" of the
    United States, a country of "supermanagers," which is "a very
    inegalitarian society, but one in which the peak of the income
    hierarchy is dominated by very high incomes from labor rather
    than by inherited wealth." See Thomas Piketty, *Capital in the
    Twenty-First Century*. Trans. Arthur Goldhammer (Cambridge:
    Harvard University Press, 2014), 265.

29 Jameson, *Archaeologies of the Future*, 147.

30 See Benjamin Kunkel, *Utopia or Bust* (New York: Verso, 2014),
    99–104.

31 See Jameson, *Archaeologies of the Future*, 148.

32 See "Background Facts on Contingent Faculty." *American
    Association of University Professors*. http://www.aaup.org/issues/
    contingency/background-facts (accessed February 9, 2016).

33 To which we can add Jameson's assertion from *The
    Geopolitical Aesthetic* that "the heist genre itself [is] always in
    one way or another an inscription of collective nonalienated
    work that passes the censor by way of its rewriting in terms of
    crime and sub-generic entertainment" (14–15).

34 See David Harvey, "Afterthoughts on Piketty's *Capital*."
    Davidharvey.org. http://davidharvey.org/2014/05/afterthoughts
    -pikettys-capital/ (accessed February 9, 2016). But Doug
    Henwood (in *Bookforum*), Thomas Frank (in *Salon*) and
    Benjamin Kunkel (in the *London Review of Books*) have also
    provided useful, and perhaps in solidarity, critiques.

35 See Jameson, *Archaeologies of the Future*, 199. See also
    Jameson, "The Antinomies of Postmodernity." *The Cultural
    Turn: Selected Writings on the Postmodern, 1983–1998*
    (London: Verso, 1998), 50. See, finally, Slavoj Žižek,
    introduction to *Mapping Ideology* (London: Verso, 1994), 1.
    This genealogy is that of "Qlipoth," who argues that the source
    of Jameson's first formulation lies in an essay by

radical science fiction critic H. Bruce Franklin, writing on J.G. Ballard. *Qlipoth*, November 11, 2009. http://qlipoth.blogspot .ca/2009/11/easier-to-imagine-end-of-world.html?m=1 (accessed February 9, 2016).

36 References are to the manuscript. Grateful thanks to Fredric Jameson for very generously sharing this text with the author.

37 Stephen Best and Sharon Marcus, "Surface Reading: An Introduction." *Representations* 108.1 (Fall 2009), 1–21, 2.

38 Here I am guided by Alison Dean's Ph.D. dissertation on photography (Department of English, Simon Fraser University, 2015).

39 See Carolyn Lesjak, "Reading Dialectically." *Criticism* 55.2 (Spring 2013), 233–277.

40 See Mary Thomas Crane, "Surface, Depth, and the Spatial Imaginary: A Cognitive Reading of *The Political Unconscious*." *Representations* 108.1 (Fall 2009), 76–97.

41 Jameson, *The Political Unconscious*, 19.

42 Bill Nichols, "Form Wars: The Political Unconscious of Formalist Theory." In *Classical Hollywood Narratives: The Paradigm Wars*, ed. Jane Gaines (Durham: Duke University Press, 1992), 49–78, 62.

43 Michael Walsh, "Jameson and 'Global Aesthetics'." In *Post-Theory: Reconstructing Film Studies*, eds David Bordwell and Noël Carroll (Madison: University of Wisconsin Press, 1996), 481–500.

44 See Matthew Flisfeder, *The Symbolic, the Sublime, and Slavoj Žižek's Theory of Film* (London: Palgrave, 2013), 12–13.

45 Tania Modleski, *The Women Who Knew Too Much: Hitchcock and Feminist Theory* (New York: Routledge, 1989), 73–86.

Chapter Two

1 Bloch, *Principle of Hope*, 348.

2 Bertolt Brecht, "Über Stoffe und Formen" (1929). In *Brecht on Theatre*, ed. J. Willett (London: Methuen, 1978), 30. Ctd. Toscano and Kinkle, *Cartographies of the Absolute*, 84.

3 See Financial Crisis Inquiry Commission, *The Financial Crisis Inquiry Report* (Washington: U.S. Government Printing Office, 2011), 129, 131.

4 Jameson discusses precisely this role of the voice-over in his forthcoming *Raymond Chandler: The Detections of Totality* (London: Verso, 2016).

5 It is no accident that for Jameson, the axiom of adaptation (and one which engages with the trope of fidelity in a sideways fashion) is that "the novel and its film adaptation must not be of equal quality." See his "Adaptation as a Philosophical Problem." In *True to the Spirit: Film Adaptation and the Question of Fidelity*, eds Colin McCabe et al. (Oxford: Oxford University Press, 2011), 214–234, 217.

6 See Jordan Belfort, *The Wolf of Wall Street* (New York: Bantam, 2013), 30.

7 See F. Scott Fitzgerald, *The Great Gatsby* (New York: Scribner's, 1953), 93.

8 Belfort, *The Wolf of Wall Street*, 59.

9 Ibid., 68.

10 Bloch, *Principle of Hope*, 347.

Conclusion

1 See Fredric Jameson, "Culture and Finance Capital." In *The Jameson Reader*, eds Michael Hardt and Kathi Weeks (Oxford: Blackwell, 2002), 255–274, 259.

2 See *Martin Scorsese: Interviews*, ed. Peter Brunette (Jackson: University of Mississippi Press, 1999), 141–142, 160. Ctd. Julie Hubbert, "'Without Music, I Would Be Lost': Scorsese, *Goodfellas*, and a New Soundtrack Practice." In *Popular Music and the New Auteur*, ed. Arved Ashby (Oxford: Oxford University Press, 2013), 31–62, 41.

FURTHER READING

On Scorsese and film criticism

Aaron Baker, ed. *A Companion to Martin Scorsese*. Oxford: Wiley
    Blackwell, 2015. As a survey of up-to-date criticism of the
    Scorsese canon, the *Companion* cannot be beat. Never afraid
    to rattle cages (Marc Raymond's take on Scorsese's *auteurism*
    is worth the price of admission), the collection offers such
    unexpected pleasures as a queer take on *The Last Temptation of
    Christ* and a feminist essay on *Goodfellas*.
David Bordwell and Nöel Carroll, eds, *Post-Theory: Reconstructing
    Film Studies*. Madison: University of Wisconsin Press, 1996.
    Bordwell and Carroll's collection of essays is diametrically
    opposed to much of what Jameson's film criticism sets out to do.
    It is, however, an important book for clarifying the terms of an
    ongoing debate in film studies, between theoretical and empirical
    approaches.
David Thompson and Ian Christie, eds, *Scorsese on Scorsese*.
    London: Faber, 1996. The essential collection of interviews
    (based on interviews at the National Film Theater in London
    in the 1980s, but updated), replete with Scorsese's anecdotes,
    justifications, and inimitable storytelling.

On Jameson and Marxist criticism

Michael Hardt and Kathi Weeks, eds, *The Jameson Reader*. London:
    Blackwell, 2000. While not, unfortunately, able to include
    Jameson's more recent writings on dialectics and utopia (a new
    edition is called for), Hardt and Weeks' anthology remains
    the best teaching collection of Jameson's work, including,
    impressively, a chunk of his chapter on interpretation in *The
    Political Unconscious*.

Sean Homer, *Fredric Jameson: Marxism, Hermeutics, Postmodernism*. London: Routledge, 1998. This is the best book on Jameson, for the simple reason that Homer never shies away from the difficulties of Jameson's concepts, difficulties that he is sometimes too quick to ascribe to a matter of style or hermeticism, rather than the matter of Jameson's object—which is the complexity of contemporary capitalism.

Alberto Toscano and Jeff Kinkle, *Cartographies of the Absolute*. London: Zero Books, 2015. Toscano and Kinkle not only provide the essential guide to films about contemporary finance, but, in their range of cultural examples are especially impressive, delving into contemporary art and video as a way of exploring Jameson's concept of "cognitive mapping" in relation to today's society of a financialized spectacle.

On Wall Street and economics

Financial Crisis Inquiry Commission, *The Financial Crisis Inquiry Report*. Washington: U.S. Government Printing Office, 2011. A surprisingly readable government report on the subprime mortgage crisis, which explains CDOs, tranches, and derivatives in terms your stockbroker wishes he could.

Doug Henwood, *Wall Street: How It Works and for Whom*. New York: Verso, 1997. For many of us, Henwood remains the most readable Marxist on financial economics. His informants range impressively from inside players to sex trade workers, and his sense of outrage is never far from the surface.

John Lanchester, *IOU: Why Everyone Owes Everyone and No-one Can Pay*. New York: Simon and Shuster, 2010. As a journalistic account of the 2007–2008 crisis, Lanchester kicks other contenders (Michael Lewis, for one) to the curb, forgoing character sketches for clear writing, trenchant analysis, and a scope that escapes the fishbowl that is Manhattan (Lanchester writes from London).

Thomas Piketty, *Capital in the Twenty-First Century*. Trans. Arthur Goldhammer. Cambridge: Harvard University Press, 2014. The blockbuster that surprised the right and pissed off the left, Piketty's book is both readable and revolutionary. What other economist combines data sets a layperson can understand with references to Balzac *and* the Disney cartoon *The Aristocats*?

INDEX